My Sight Words Workbook

This book belongs to:

For general information on our other products and services or to obtain technical support, please contact our Customer Care Department within the United States at (866) 744-2665, or outside the United States at (510) 253-0500.

Rockridge Press publishes its books in a variety of electronic and print formats. Some content that appears in print may not be available in electronic books, and vice versa.

Interior and Cover Designer: Stephanie Sumulong

Art Producer: Sara Feinstein

Editor: Kristen Depken

Production Editor: Andrew Yackira

Photography: All images used under license from Shutterstock.com and iStock.com.

Illustrations: © Robin Boyer, 2019

ISBN: Print 978-1-64152-586-2

My Sight Words Workbook

101

High-Frequency Words
Plus Games & Activities!

LAURIN BRAINARD

ROCKRIDGE
PRESS

Note to Parents

Welcome to the wonderful world of sight words! This workbook will teach your child how to read the first 101 sight words from the Fry word list in a fun and engaging way. The Fry words are introduced in order of the words most commonly encountered in print. Since sight words are used so often when reading, it is important that children can identify these words by "sight," or instantly. In addition, sight words do not always follow the rules of phonics, so children cannot rely on blending and decoding when identifying these words.

As a first grade teacher and the mother of two young children, I have personally seen the difference in a child's ability to read once they can identify the first 101 sight words. Each year in my classroom I teach a group of children how to read. After my students learn their sight words, they are well on their way to becoming successful independent readers. It is so rewarding to see their little eyes light up with excitement the first time they read a book on their own.

All the activities in this book are designed to grab and hold your child's attention. Every child learns at a different rate, so spend as much time as needed on each sight word. Each page includes a practice section where your child will trace and write the word. Then your child will complete two fun activities that offer additional practice in learning the new sight word. For the last activity on each page your child will unscramble the word and paste it in a sentence.

Work on one sight word at a time. You will know your child has mastered a sight word when he or she is able to quickly identify the word without trying to sound out each letter. Once a child has completed the first 101 sight word pages, he or she is ready to do the bonus games and activities at the end of the book. I hope you have a wonderful time helping your child learn to read sight words.

Let's begin!

Laurin

Way to Go!

After completing each activity, color a star to track how much you've done!

1 2 3 4

5 6 7 8 9 10

11 12 13 14 15 16

17 18 19 20 21 22

23 24 25 26 27 28

29	30	31	32	33	34
35	36	37	38	39	40
41	42	43	44	45	46
47	48	49	50	51	52
53	54	55	56	57	58
59	60	61	62	63	64
65	66	67	68	69	70

71	72	73	74	75	76
77	78	79	80	81	82
83	84	85	86	87	88
89	90	91	92	93	94
95	96	97	98	99	100
101					

Say the word. Then trace the word.

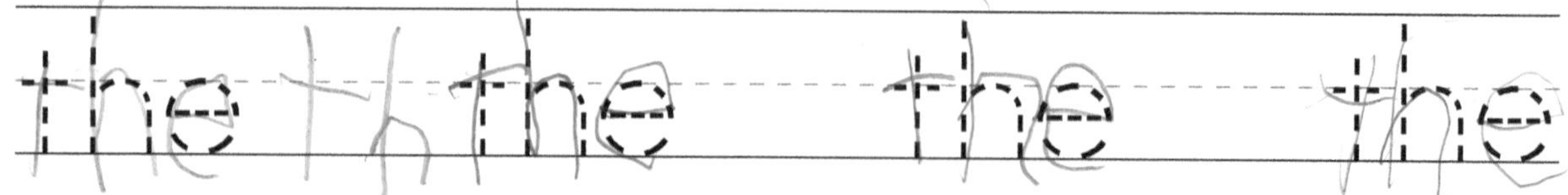

Write the word.

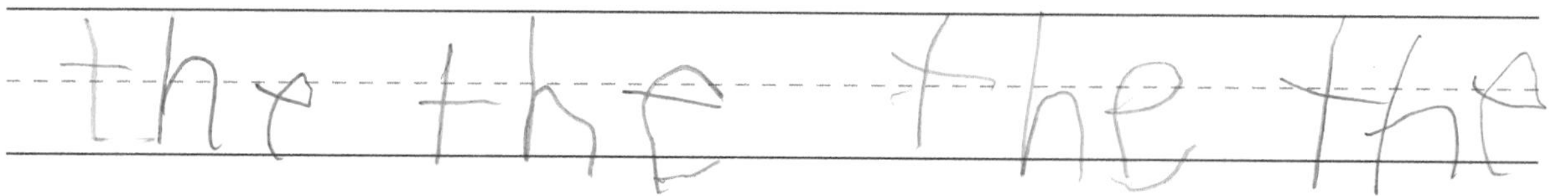

Color each space that has the word the.

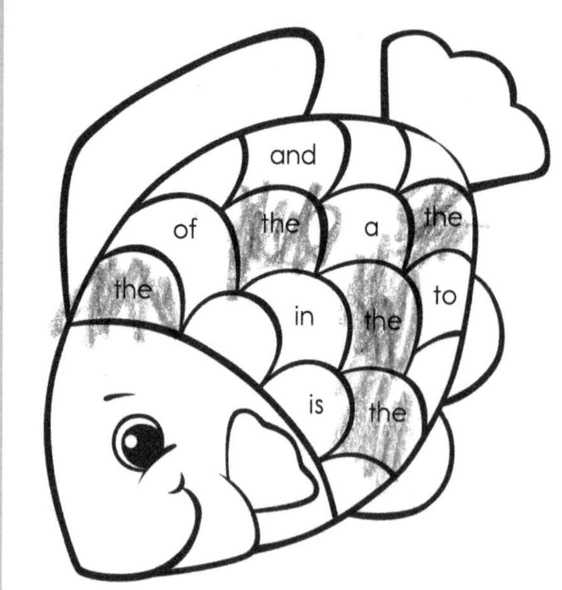

Find the word the. Draw a line to connect the letters.

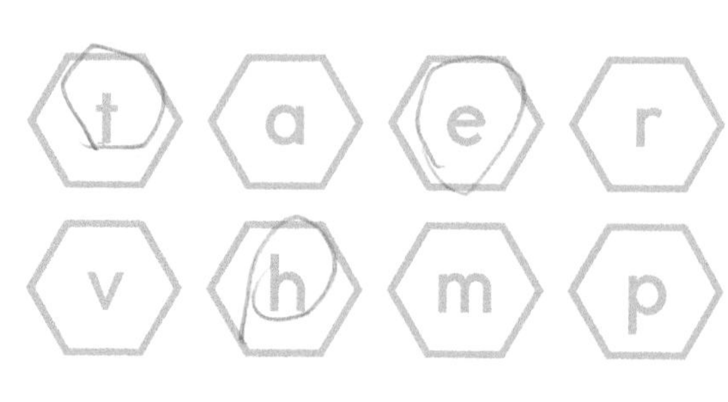

Cut out the letters at the bottom of the page. Then paste them in the correct order to complete the sentence.

___ dog is brown.

e T h

The word of makes an uv sound as in oven.

Say the word. Then trace the word.

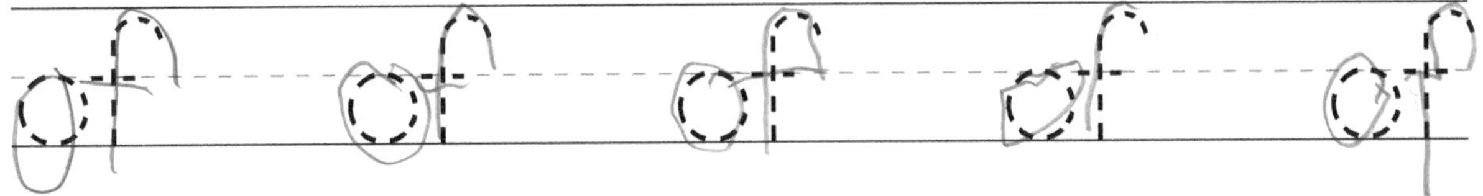

Write the word.

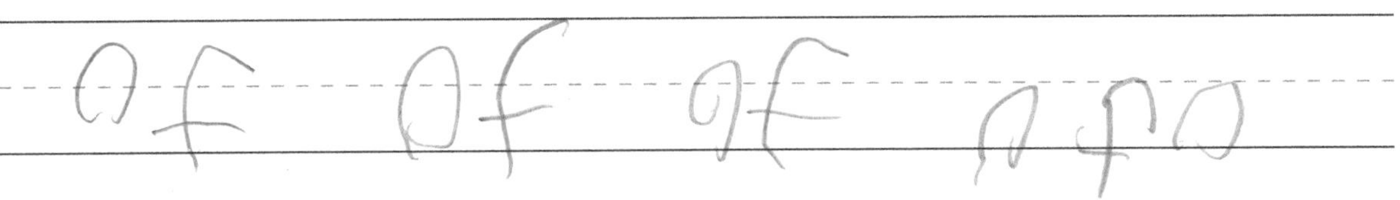

Begin at the red arrow. Connect the dots to finish the picture.

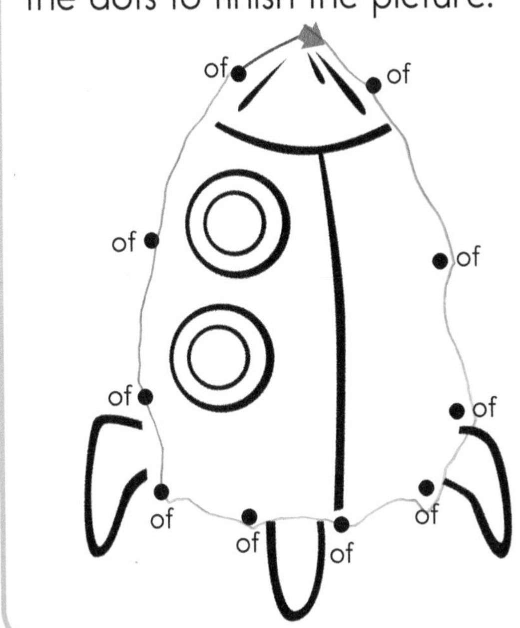

Complete the maze. Color the circles that have the word of.

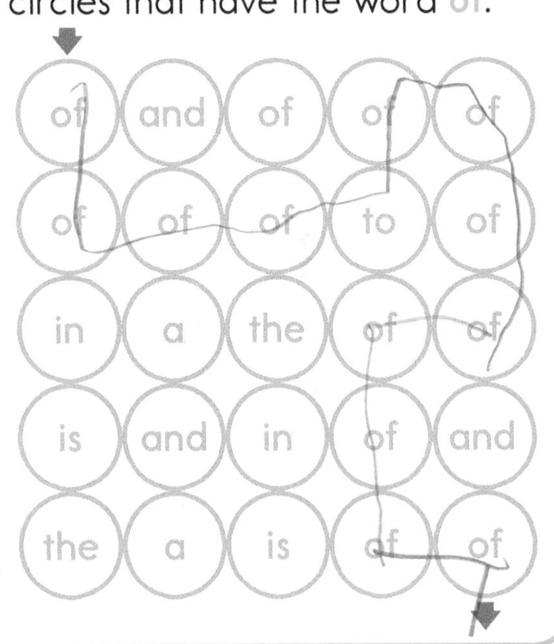

Cut out the letters at the bottom of the page. Then paste them in the correct order to complete the sentence.

I have a cup  milk.

and

The word **and** has three letters and three sounds: **short a – n – d.**

Say the word. Then trace the word.

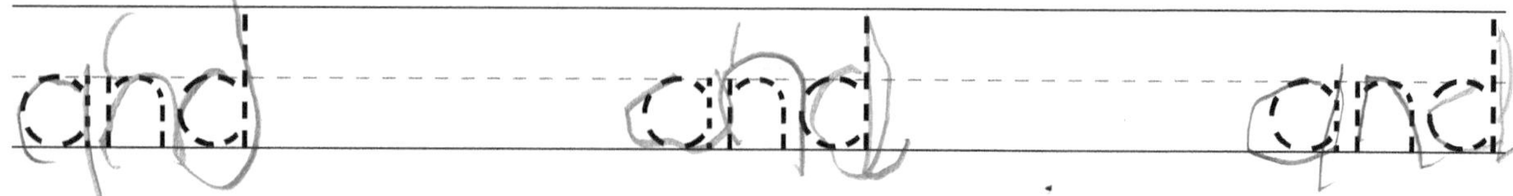

Write the word.

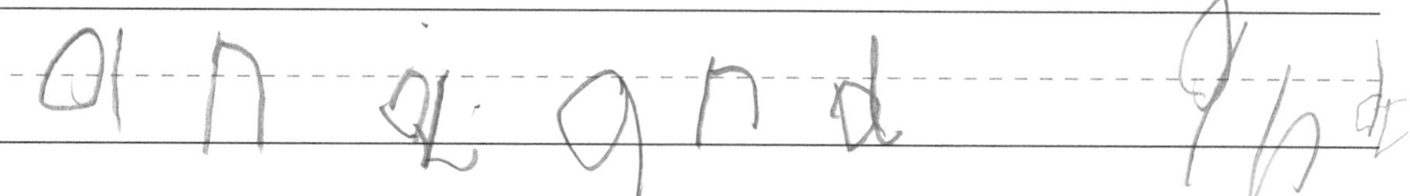

Color each space that has the word **and**.

Fill in the missing letters to write the word **and**.

a __ __   __ n __

a __ d   __ nd

__ __ d   an __

Cut out the letters at the bottom of the page. Then paste them in the correct order to complete the sentence.

Do you like my hat __ __ __ scarf?

n d a

Say the word. Then trace the word.

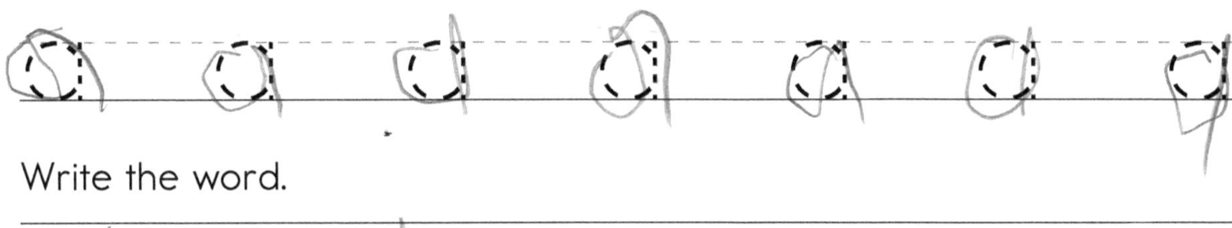

Write the word.

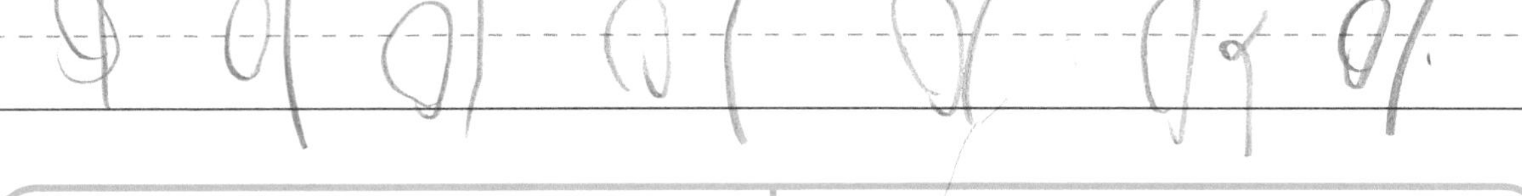

Circle each apple that has the word a.

How many times can you find the word a?

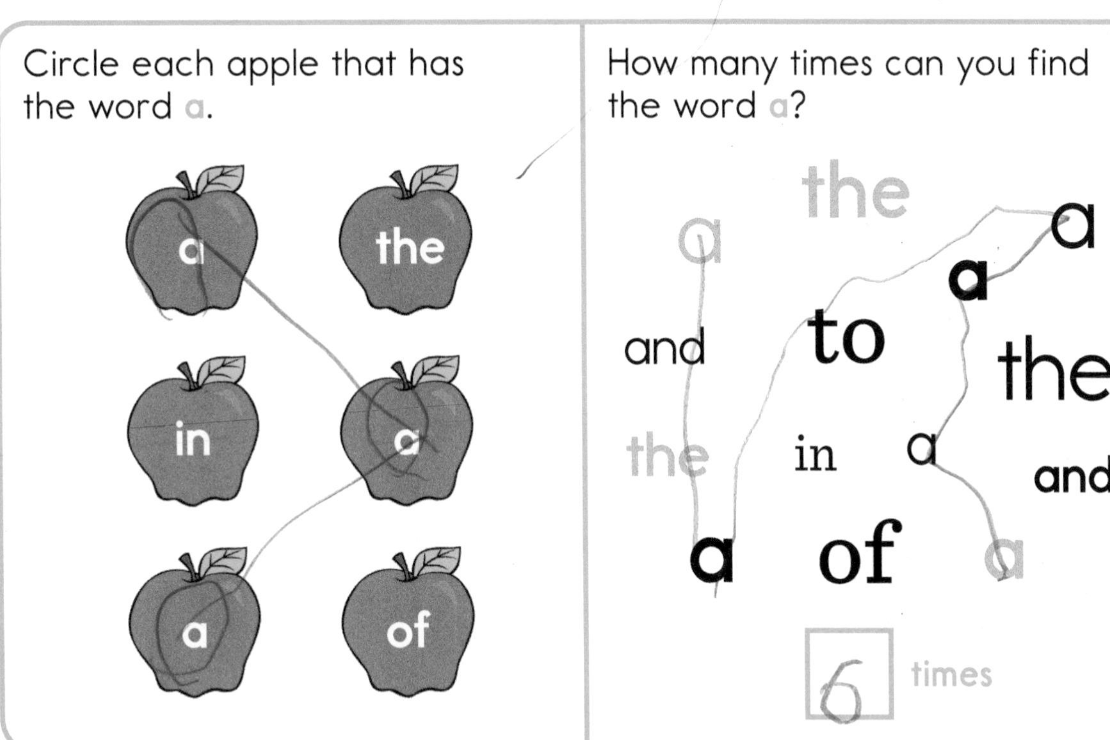

Cut out the letters at the bottom of the page. Then paste them in the correct order to complete the sentence.

May I have ___ pink popsicle, please?

a

to

The o in to makes an oo sound, like in boo.

Say the word. Then trace the word.

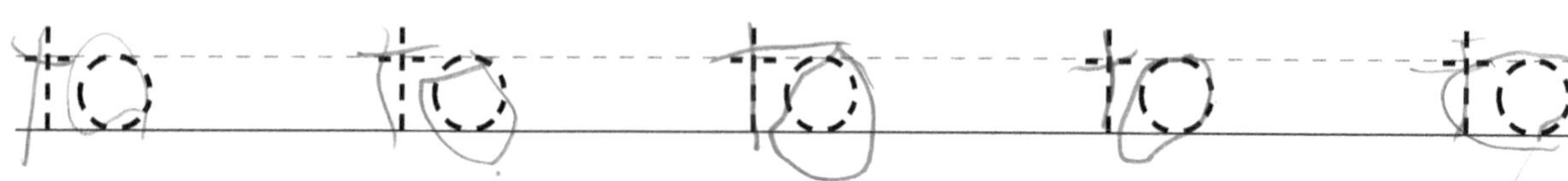

Write the word.

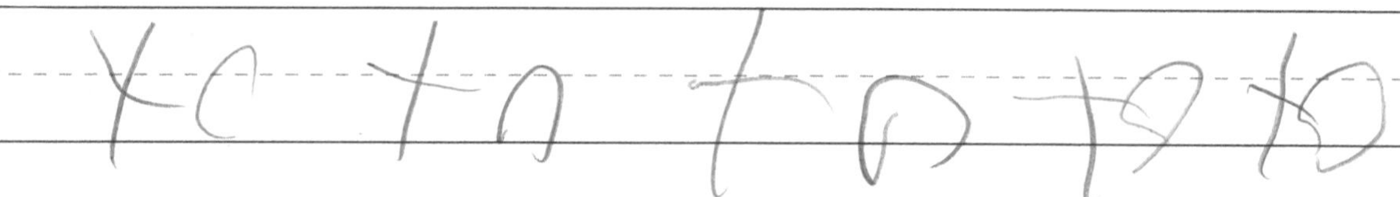

Draw a line to match each word.

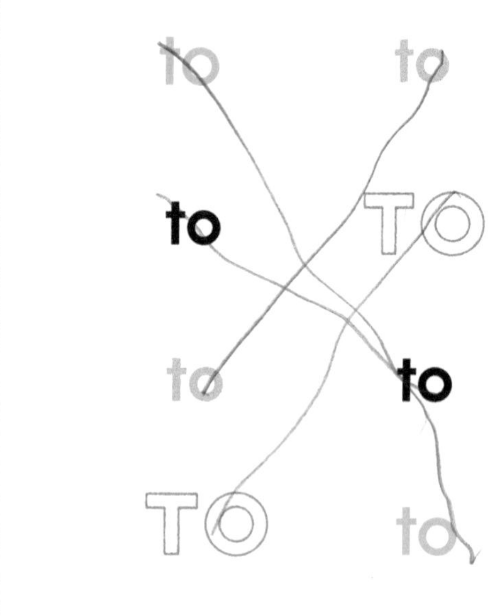

Find and circle the word to three times.

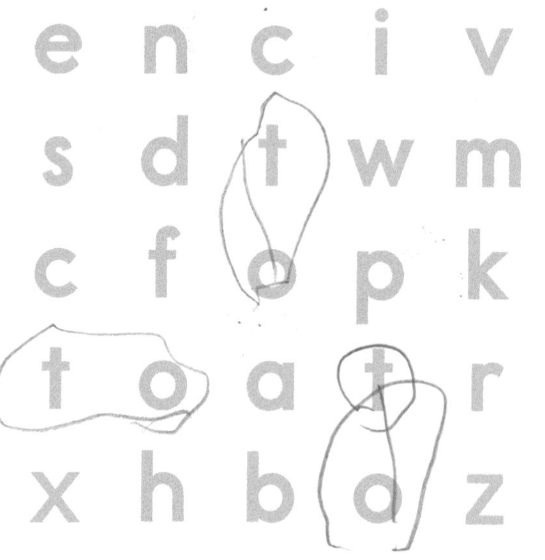

Cut out the letters at the bottom of the page. Then paste them in the correct order to complete the sentence.

I like ☐☐ read.

✂ o t

Say the word. Then trace the word.

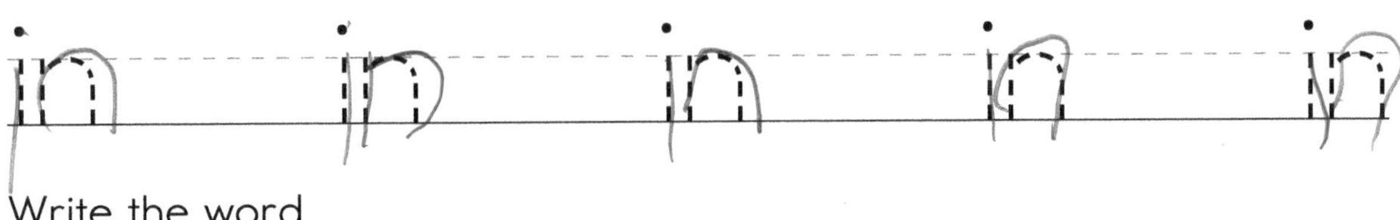

Write the word.

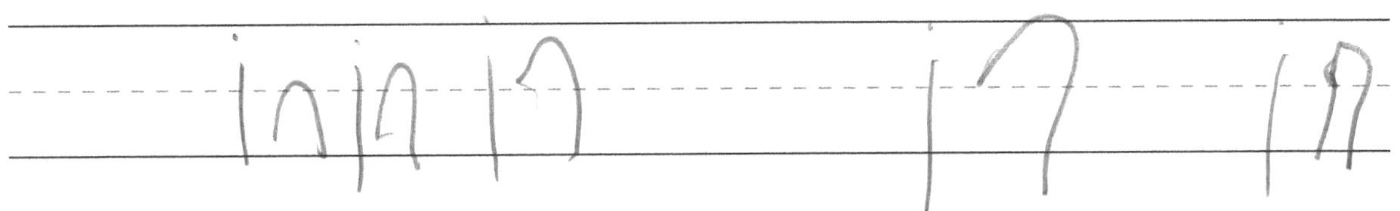

Color each space that has the word in.

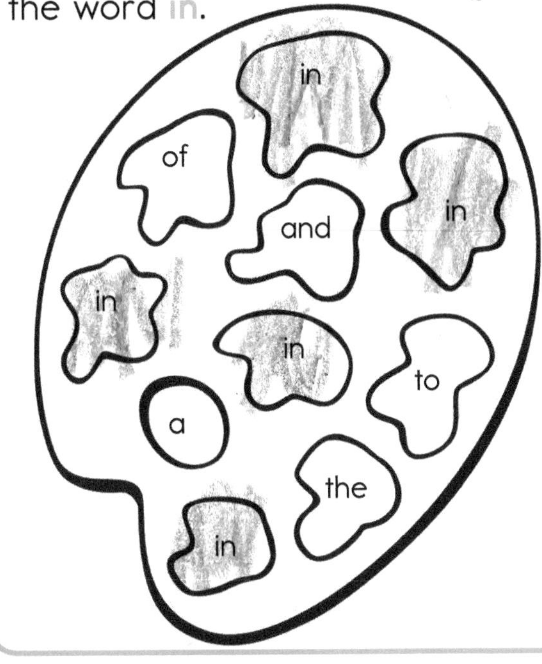

Find the word in. Draw a line to connect the letters.

Cut out the letters at the bottom of the page. Then paste them in the correct order to complete the sentence.

The puppies are 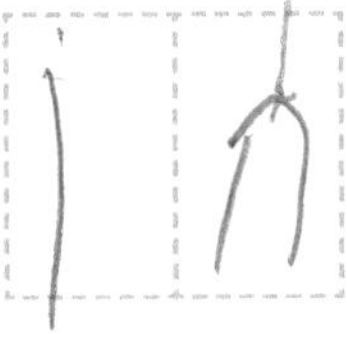 the basket.

n i

is

Say the word. Then trace the word.

is is is is is

Write the word.

Begin at the red arrow. Connect the dots to finish the picture.

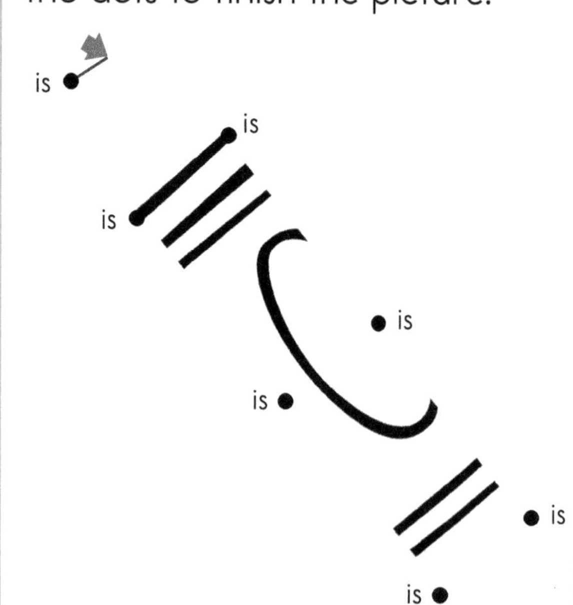

Complete the maze. Color the circles that have the word is.

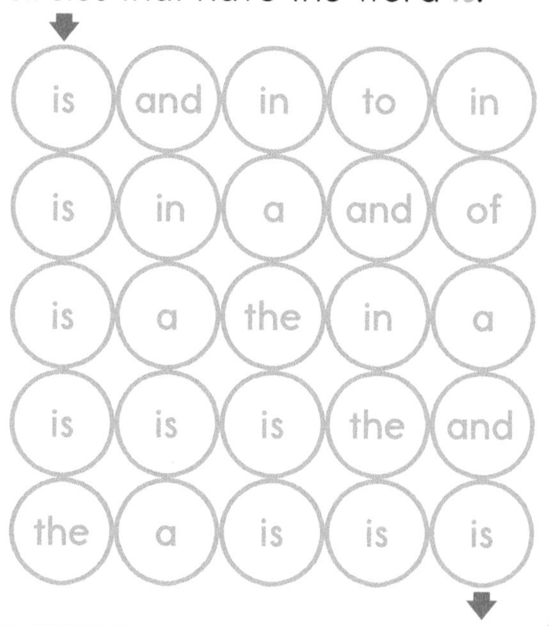

Cut out the letters at the bottom of the page. Then paste them in the correct order to complete the sentence.

This ☐☐ my friend.

s i

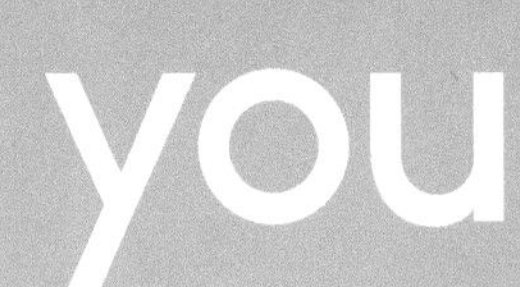

Say the word. Then trace the word.

you you you

Write the word.

Color each space that has the word you.

Fill in the missing letters to write the word you.

y_ _   _o_

y_u   _ou

_ _u   yo_

Cut out the letters at the bottom of the page. Then paste them in the correct order to complete the sentence.

Do 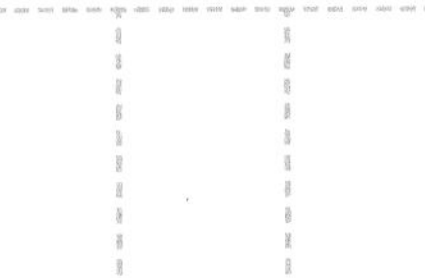 like pizza?

o u y

that

That rhymes with mat and cat.

Say the word. Then trace the word.

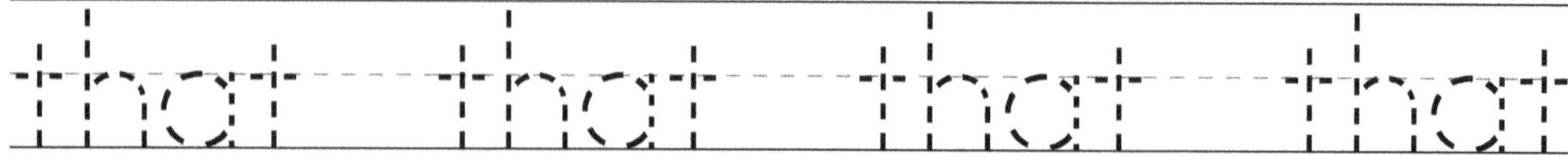

Write the word.

Circle each peach that has the word that.

How many times can you find the word that?

that that and
in you
that to that
the that in that
that of to

times

Cut out the letters at the bottom of the page. Then paste them in the correct order to complete the sentence.

cake looks delicious!

a T h t

Put the short i and the t sounds together to make the word it.

Say the word. Then trace the word.

it it it it it

Write the word.

Draw a line to match each word.

IT	it
it	IT
it	**it**
it	it

Find and circle the word it three times.

u	m	f	i	g
s	d	z	k	t
i	f	r	q	k
t	a	i	t	r
x	h	b	v	w

Cut out the letters at the bottom of the page. Then paste them in the correct order to complete the sentence.

Is ___ raining?

t i

he

Say the word. Then trace the word.

he he he he he

Write the word.

Color each space that has the word he.

Find the word he. Draw a line to connect the letters.

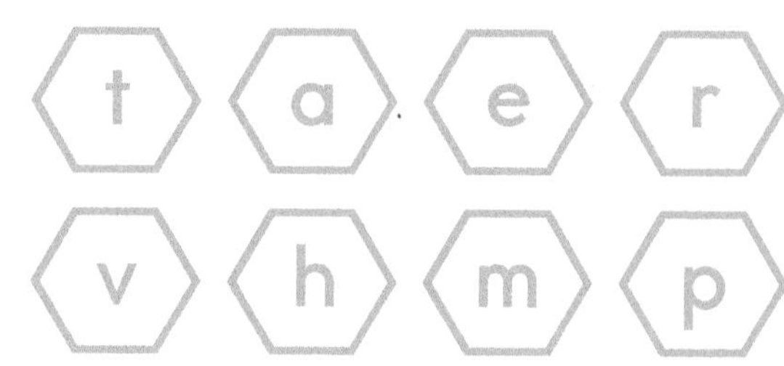

Cut out the letters at the bottom of the page. Then paste them in the correct order to complete the sentence.

e H

Say the word. Then trace the word.

was was was was

Write the word.

Begin at the red arrow. Connect the dots to finish the picture.

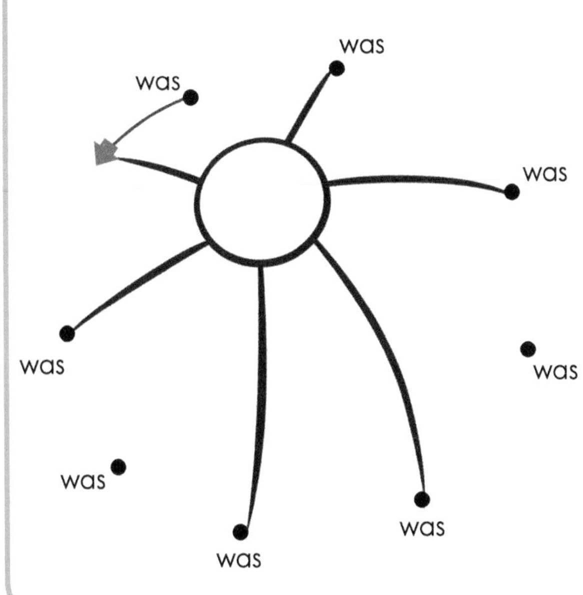

Complete the maze. Color the circles that have the word was.

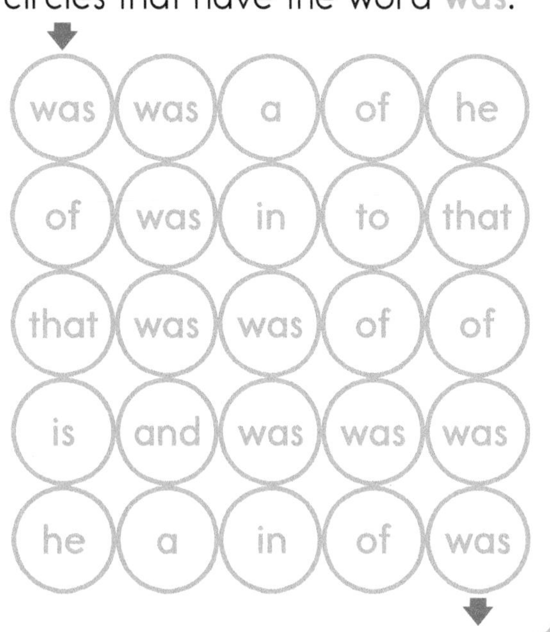

Cut out the letters at the bottom of the page. Then paste them in the correct order to complete the sentence.

Mom said I ☐☐☐ a cute baby.

s w a

for

The word for sounds just like the number 4.

Say the word. Then trace the word.

for for for for

Write the word.

Color each space that has the word for.

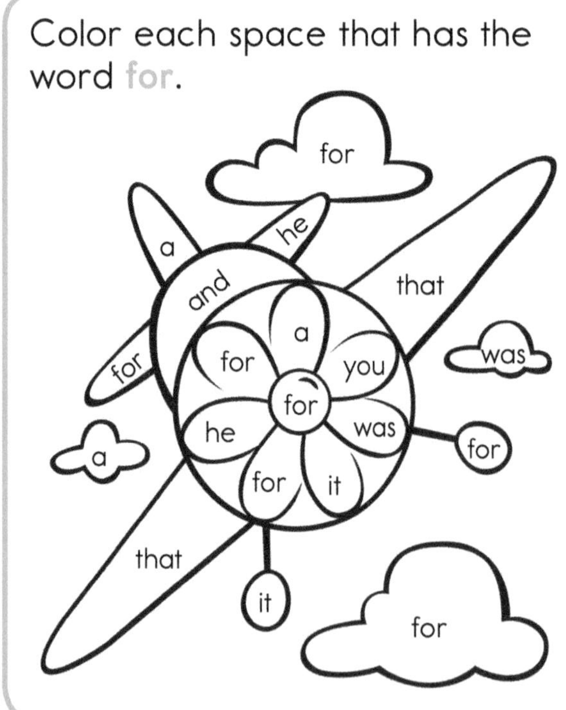

Fill in the missing letters to write the word for.

f__ _o_

f_r _or

__r fo_

Cut out the letters at the bottom of the page. Then paste them in the correct order to complete the sentence.

Crayons are ___ coloring!

o r f

Say the word. Then trace the word.

on on on on on

Write the word.

Circle each cherry that has the word on.

How many times can you find the word on?

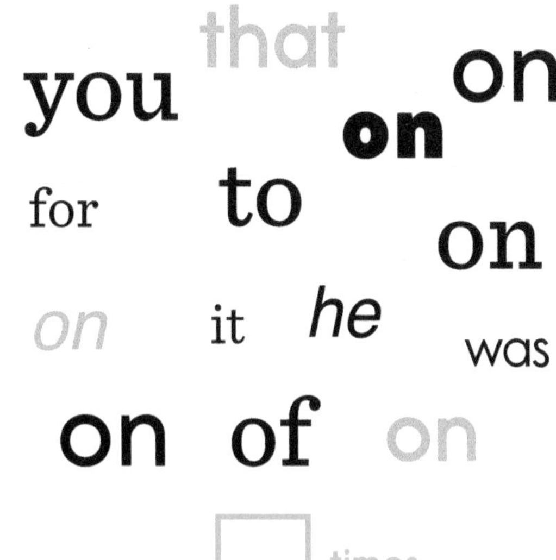

Cut out the letters at the bottom of the page. Then paste them in the correct order to complete the sentence.

The cat is ☐☐ a skateboard.

are

Say the word. Then trace the word.

are are are are

Write the word.

Draw a line to match each word.		Find and circle the word are three times.				
are	are	a	b	a	g	k
ARE	are	r	d	t	r	m
are	are	e	p	o	y	e
are	ARE	t	d	a	r	e
		u	h	b	s	z

Cut out the letters at the bottom of the page. Then paste them in the correct order to complete the sentence.

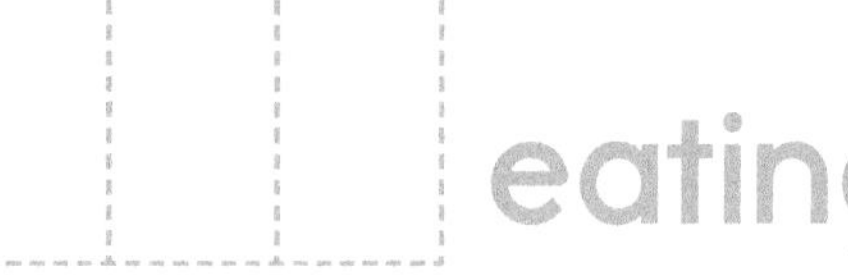

We ☐☐☐ eating popcorn. Yum!

r a e

The s in as
makes a z sound,
like in fuzz.

Say the word. Then trace the word.

as as as as as

Write the word.

Color each space that has the word as.

Find the word as. Draw a line to connect the letters.

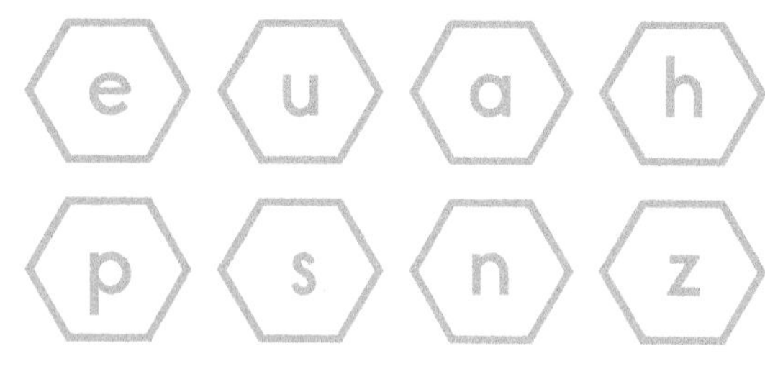

Cut out the letters at the bottom of the page. Then paste them in the correct order to complete the sentence.

Kitty's fur is [ ][ ] white [ ][ ] a marshmallow.

s a   a s

In with, the letters t and h blend together to make one sound.

Say the word. Then trace the word.

with with with

Write the word.

Begin at the red arrow. Connect the dots to finish the picture.

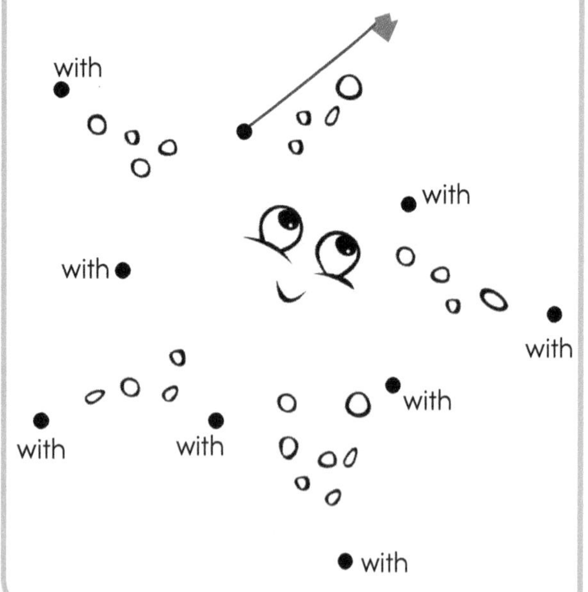

Complete the maze. Color the circles that have the word with.

Cut out the letters at the bottom of the page. Then paste them in the correct order to complete the sentence.

I like french fries

ketchup.

t i h w

Say the word. Then trace the word.

his his his his

Write the word.

Color each space that has the word his.

Find and circle the word his three times.

f	h	i	s	w
t	i	u	x	n
d	s	h	q	l
u	p	b	i	s
y	i	c	p	s

Cut out the letters at the bottom of the page. Then paste them in the correct order to complete the sentence.

He can tie 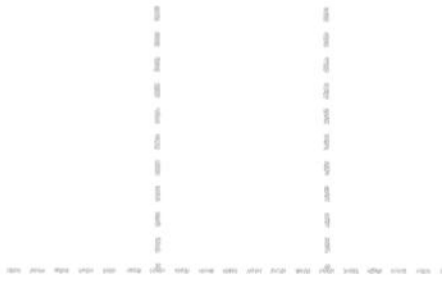 shoes.

i h s

Say the word. Then trace the word.

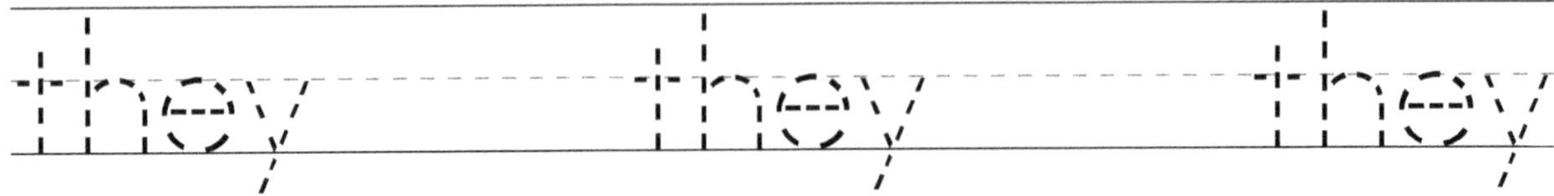

Write the word.

Circle each chick that has the word they.

Fill in the missing letters to write the word they.

t_ _ _ _ _e_

t_e_ _ _ey

_ _ _y th_ _

Cut out the letters at the bottom of the page. Then paste them in the correct order to complete the sentence.

 wear glasses.

h y e T

I

Say the word. Then trace the word.

I I I I I I

Write the word.

Draw a line to match each word.

I	I
I	I
I	I
I	I

How many times can you find the word I?

a I I is and you I is they I are I his I on

times

Cut out the letters at the bottom of the page. Then paste them in the correct order to complete the sentence.

am very happy!

I

at

Say the word. Then trace the word.

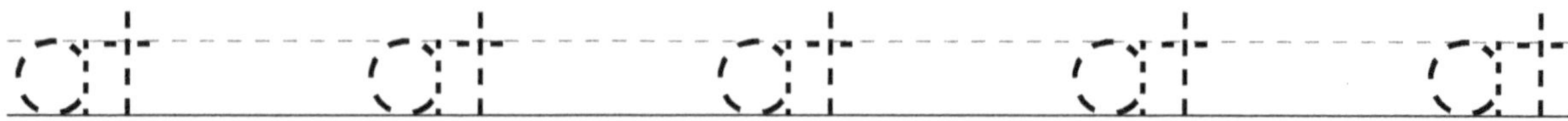

Write the word.

Color each space that has the word at.

Find the word at. Draw a line to connect the letters.

Cut out the letters at the bottom of the page. Then paste them in the correct order to complete the sentence.

Is that fish

looking  me?

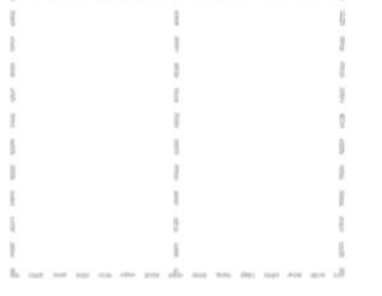

The e in be makes a long e sound, like in free.

Say the word. Then trace the word.

be be be be be

Write the word.

Begin at the red arrow. Connect the dots to finish the picture.

Complete the maze. Color the circles that have the word be.

Cut out the letters at the bottom of the page. Then paste them in the correct order to complete the sentence.

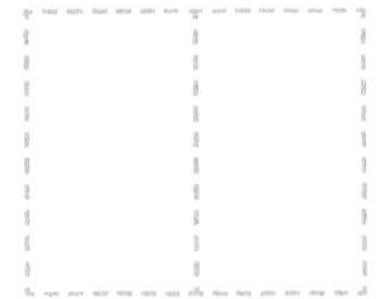

yourself!

e B

this

Say the word. Then trace the word.

this this this this

Write the word.

Color each space that has the word this.

Fill in the missing letters to write the word this.

t___ _h__

t__s __is

___s th__

Cut out the letters at the bottom of the page. Then paste them in the correct order to complete the sentence.

Wow! Is 

for me?

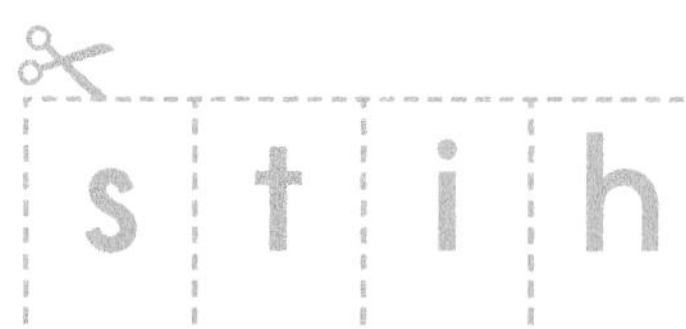

In the word **have**, the **e** is silent.

Say the word. Then trace the word.

have have have

Write the word.

Circle each blueberry that has the word **have**.

How many times can you find the word **have**?

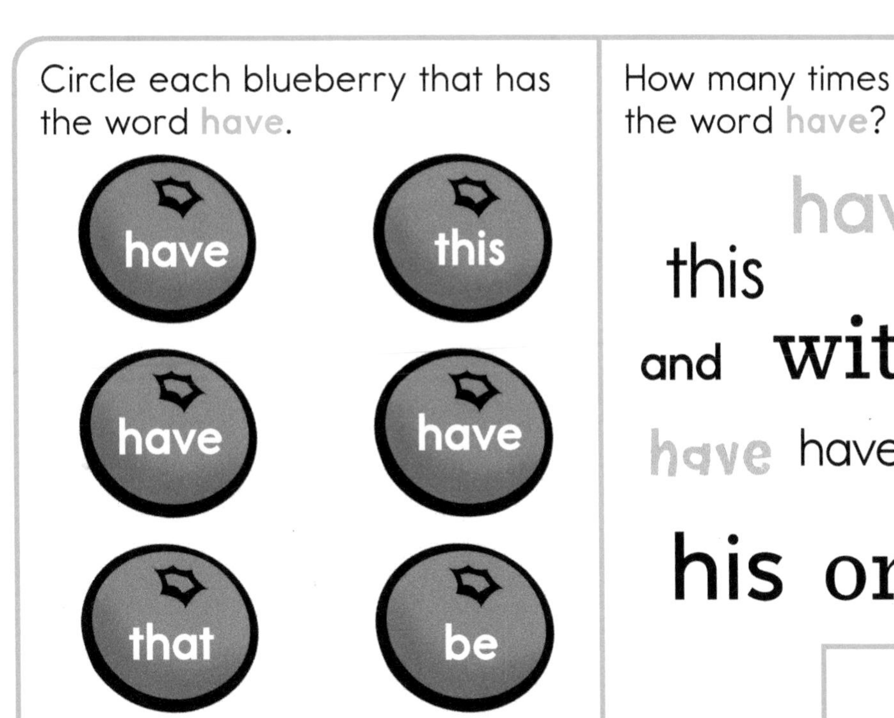

have at this be and with they have have are have his on as

☐ times

Cut out the letters at the bottom of the page. Then paste them in the correct order to complete the sentence.

I ☐☐☐☐ a green lunch box.

from

Say the word. Then trace the word.

from from from

Write the word.

Draw a line to match each word.

from from

from FROM

from from

FROM from

Find and circle the word from three times.

f	o	d	j	w
t	r	u	x	f
d	g	o	t	r
f	r	o	m	o
y	i	c	p	m

Cut out the letters at the bottom of the page. Then paste them in the correct order to complete the sentence.

These tomatoes are

____ our garden.

o f m r

Say the word. Then trace the word.

Write the word.

Color each space that has the word or.

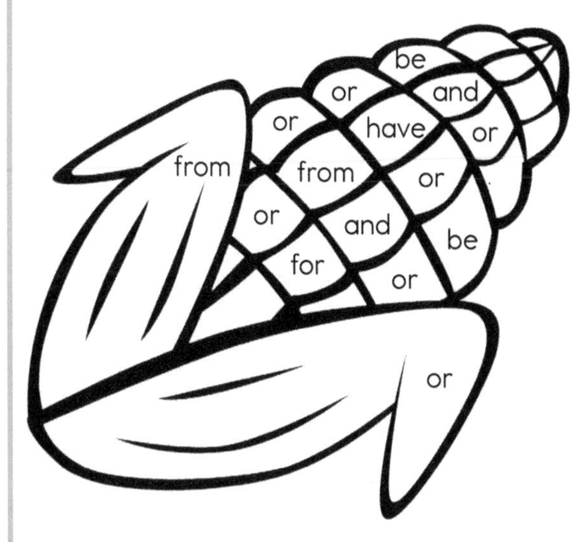

Find the word or. Draw a line to connect the letters.

Cut out the letters at the bottom of the page. Then paste them in the correct order to complete the sentence.

Do you want chocolate,

vanilla, [ ] [ ] both?

The word one sounds just like the word won.

Say the word. Then trace the word.

one one one one

Write the word.

Begin at the red arrow. Connect the dots to finish the picture.

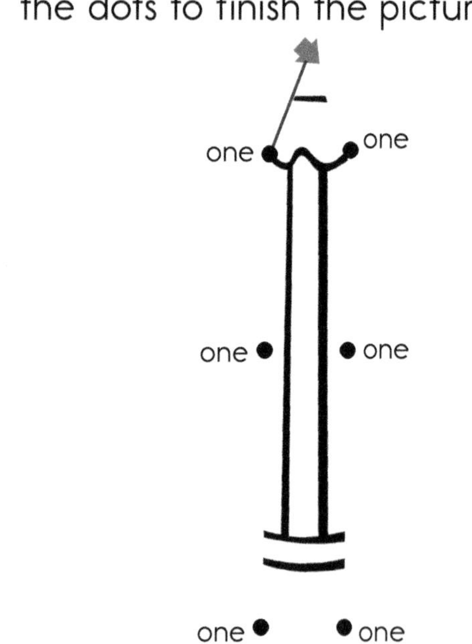

Complete the maze. Color the circles that have the word one.

Cut out the letters at the bottom of the page. Then paste them in the correct order to complete the sentence.

I have ___ special teddy bear.

e o n

Had rhymes with glad.

Say the word. Then trace the word.

had had had had

Write the word.

Color each space that has the word had.

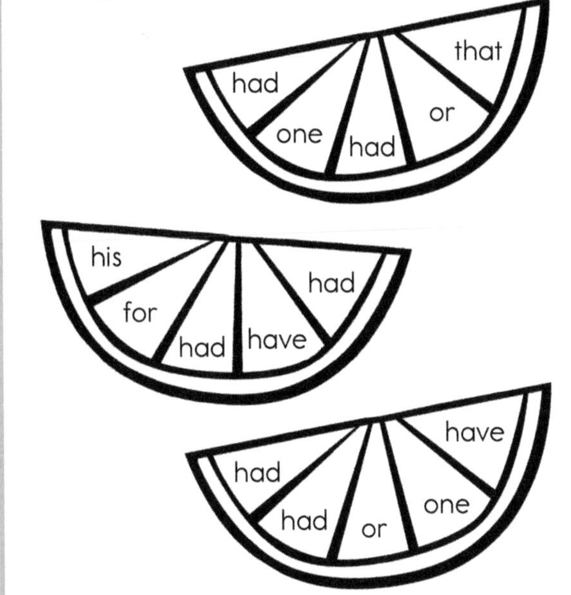

Fill in the missing letters to write the word had.

h__ _a_

h_d _ad

__d ha_

Cut out the letters at the bottom of the page. Then paste them in the correct order to complete the sentence.

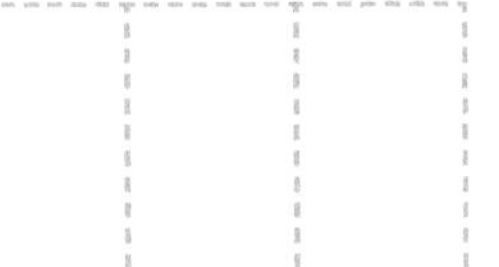

We ___ fun at the beach.

d a h

by

The letter y in by makes a long i sound, as in hi.

Say the word. Then trace the word.

by by by by by

Write the word.

Circle each heart that has the word by.

How many times can you find the word by?

by had one or from by a be this in by and at they by

☐ times

Cut out the letters at the bottom of the page. Then paste them in the correct order to complete the sentence.

I can do this all ☐☐ myself!

y b

Words rhymes with birds.

Say the word. Then trace the word.

Write the word.

Draw a line to match each word.		Find and circle the word words three times.
words	words	w o r d s
WORDS	**words**	o o u x n
words	words	r g r q l
words	WORDS	d p b d s
		s i c z s

Cut out the letters at the bottom of the page. Then paste them in the correct order to complete the sentence.

I can write lots of _ _ _ _ _.

r o d s w

The word but rhymes with nut.

Say the word. Then trace the word.

but but but but

Write the word.

Color each space that has the word but.

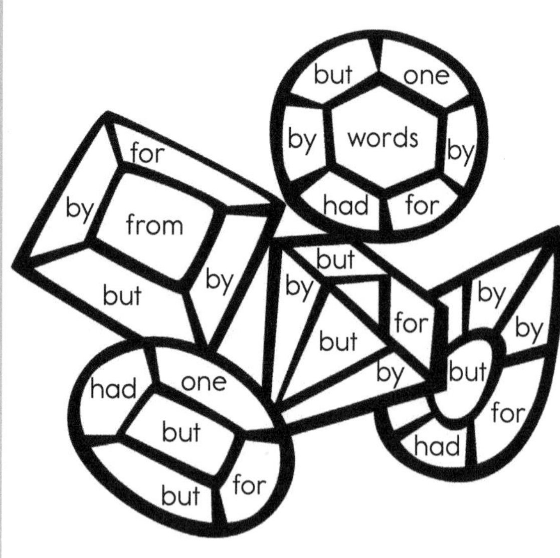

Find the word but. Draw a line to connect the letters.

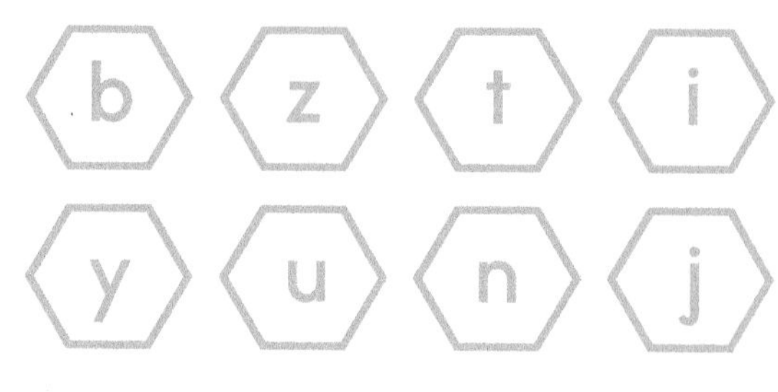

Cut out the letters at the bottom of the page. Then paste them in the correct order to complete the sentence.

Painting is messy,

[ ] [ ] [ ] it is fun!

u b t

The letter o in not makes a short o sound, like in pot.

Say the word. Then trace the word.

not not not not

Write the word.

Begin at the red arrow. Connect the dots to finish the picture.

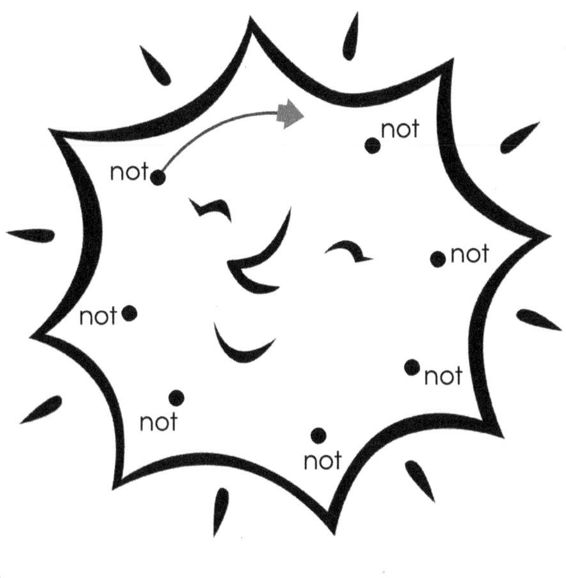

Complete the maze. Color the circles that have the word not.

Cut out the letters at the bottom of the page. Then paste them in the correct order to complete the sentence.

She is  hungry.

The letter h in what is silent.

Say the word. Then trace the word.

what what what

Write the word.

Color each space that has the word what.

Fill in the missing letters to write the word what.

w_ _ _ _h_ _

w_ _t _ _at

_ _ _t wh_ _

Cut out the letters at the bottom of the page. Then paste them in the correct order to complete the sentence.

Hello, 

is your name?

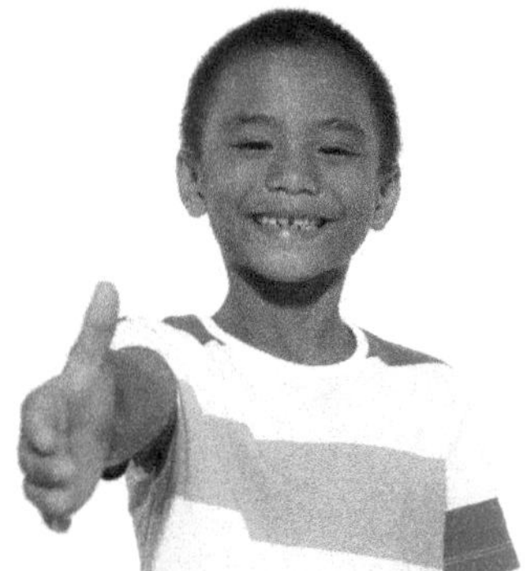

Say the word. Then trace the word.

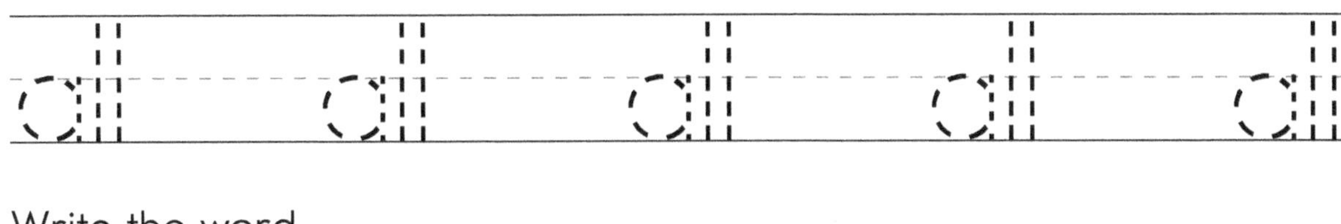

Write the word.

Circle each leaf that has the word all.

How many times can you find the word all?

all not by all
what words had
or one all all
all from all

 times

Cut out the letters at the bottom of the page. Then paste them in the correct order to complete the sentence.

___ of the animals are in the barn.

were

Say the word. Then trace the word.

were were were

Write the word.

Draw a line to match each word.		Find and circle the word were three times.
WERE	were	f o d j w
were	WERE	t w e r e
were	**were**	d g e q r
were	were	u p b r e
		y i c o e

Cut out the letters at the bottom of the page. Then paste them in the correct order to complete the sentence.

The horses 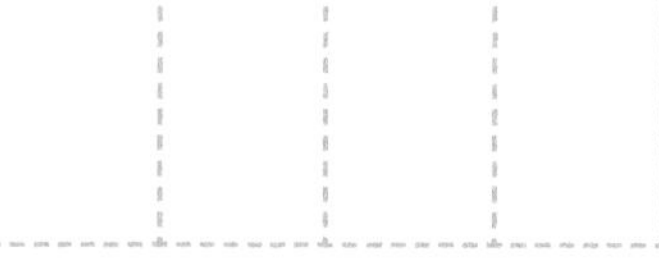

running earlier.

e r w e

Say the word. Then trace the word.

we we we we we

Write the word.

Color each space that has the word we.

Find the word we. Draw a line to connect the letters.

Cut out the letters at the bottom of the page. Then paste them in the correct order to complete the sentence.

like to jump rope.

e W

In when, the letters w and h blend together to make the w sound.

Say the word. Then trace the word.

when when when

Write the word.

Begin at the red arrow. Connect the dots to finish the picture.

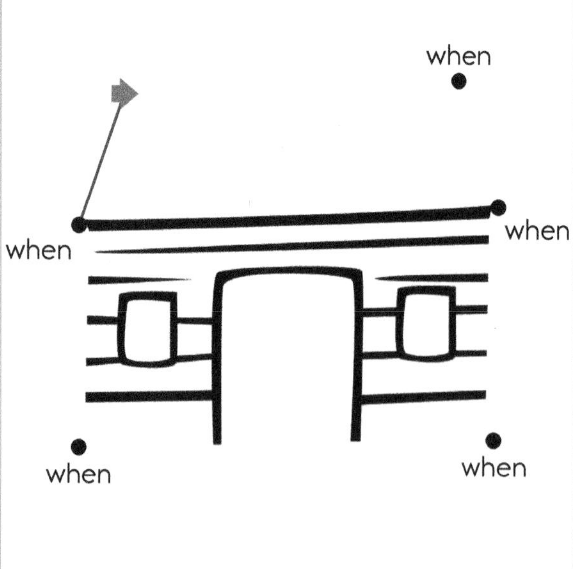

Complete the maze. Color the circles that have the word when.

Cut out the letters at the bottom of the page. Then paste them in the correct order to complete the sentence.

we get there?

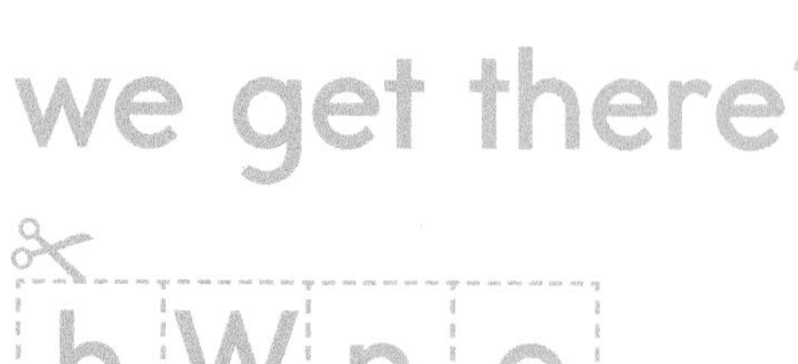

The word your has four letters, but only two sounds: y – or.

Say the word. Then trace the word.

your your your your

Write the word.

Color each space that has the word your.

Fill in the missing letters to write the word your.

y___ _o__

y__r __ur

___r yo__

Cut out the letters at the bottom of the page. Then paste them in the correct order to complete the sentence.

Put on ____ jacket.

o u y r

can

Say the word. Then trace the word.

can can can can

Write the word.

Circle each book that has the word can.

can your
when can
we can

How many times can you find the word can?

when can can we what not but can your not can were of all

☐ times

Cut out the letters at the bottom of the page. Then paste them in the correct order to complete the sentence.

Look what I ☐☐☐ do!

✂

a c n

Say the word. Then trace the word.

said said said said

Write the word.

Draw a line to match each word.

said	said
said	SAID
said	**said**
SAID	said

Find and circle the word said three times.

f	s	a	i	d
s	e	u	x	s
f	a	n	q	a
v	o	i	u	i
y	g	c	d	d

Cut out the letters at the bottom of the page. Then paste them in the correct order to complete the sentence.

"I love veggies!"

she ☐☐☐☐.

a s d i

The word there sounds just like the word their.

Say the word. Then trace the word.

there there there

Write the word.

Color each space that has the word there.

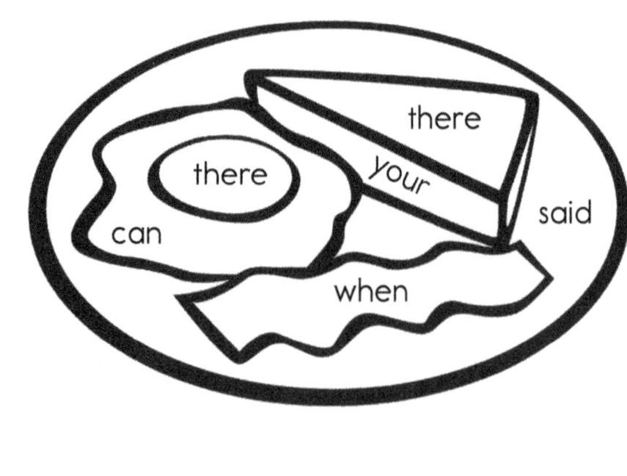

Find the word there. Draw a line to connect the letters.

Cut out the letters at the bottom of the page. Then paste them in the correct order to complete the sentence.

Do you see the bird over ____ ?

e h t r e

Say the word. Then trace the word.

use use use use

Write the word.

Begin at the red arrow. Connect the dots to finish the picture.

Complete the maze. Color the circles that have the word use.

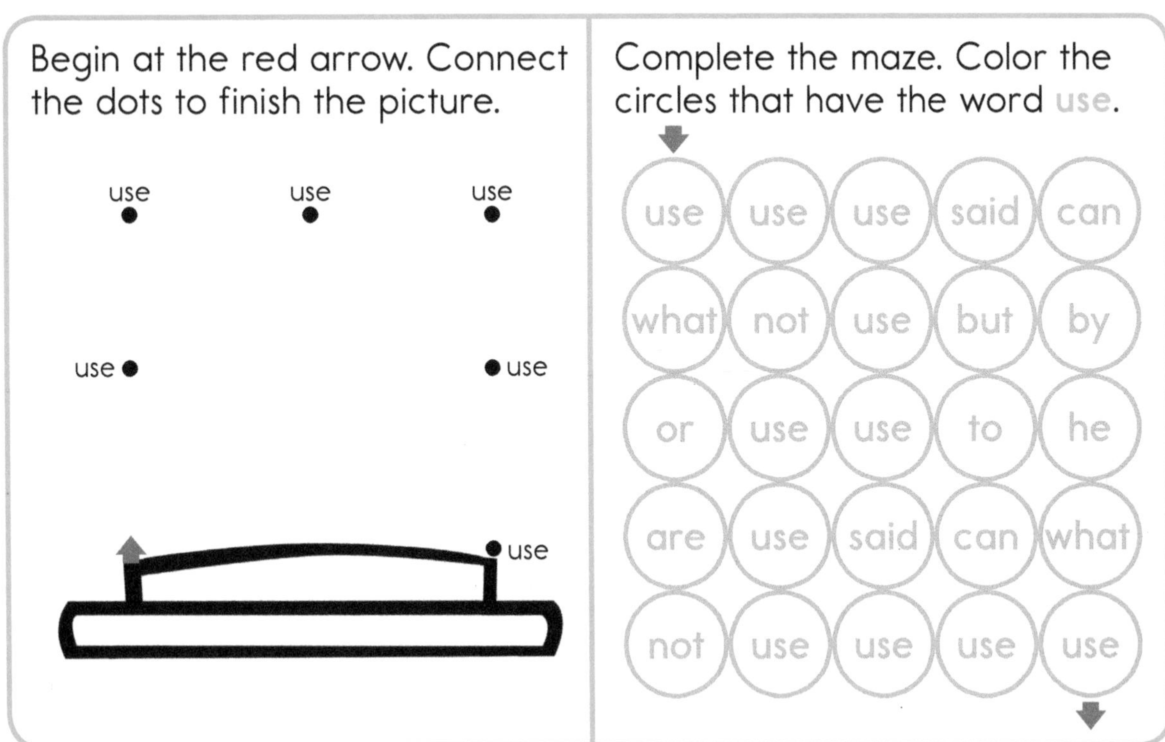

Cut out the letters at the bottom of the page. Then paste them in the correct order to complete the sentence.

an

Say the word. Then trace the word.

Write the word.

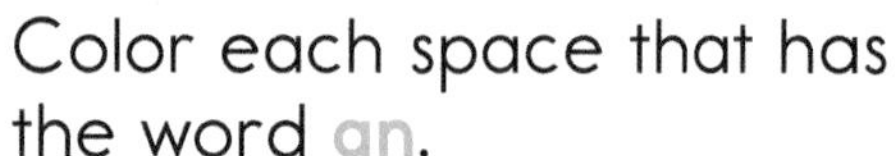

Color each space that has the word an.

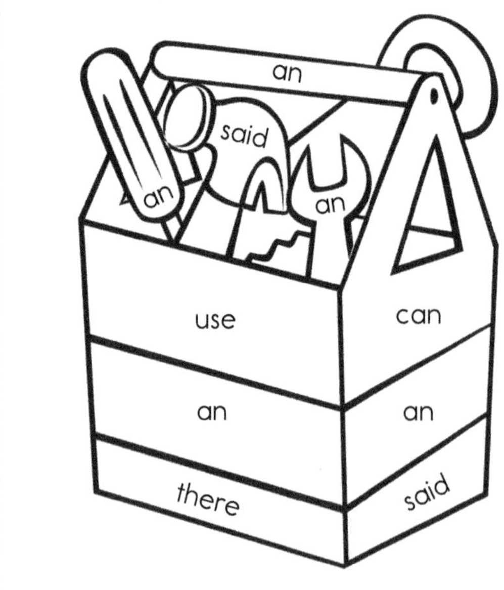

Find and circle the word an three times.

a	n	c	i	v
s	d	t	a	m
c	f	o	n	k
t	o	a	t	r
x	h	b	n	z

Cut out the letters at the bottom of the page. Then paste them in the correct order to complete the sentence.

I can eat  apple.

n a

Say the word. Then trace the word.

each each each

Write the word.

Color each flag that has the word each.

each an use each there each

How many times can you find the word each?

an each if use each each can there if an and each of said

times

Cut out the letters at the bottom of the page. Then paste them in the correct order to complete the sentence.

I smelled ____ flower.

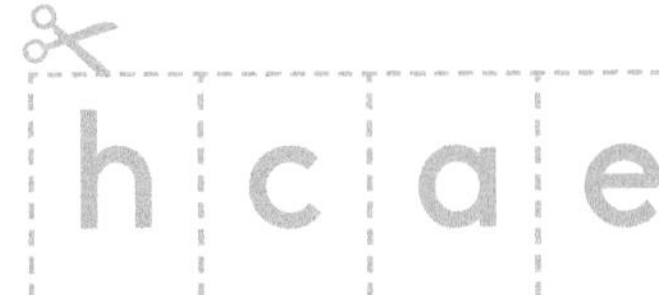

Say the word. Then trace the word.

which which which

Write the word.

Draw a line to match each word.

which	which
which	WHICH
which	**which**
WHICH	which

Find and circle the word which three times.

w	o	d	j	w
t	h	u	x	h
d	g	i	q	i
u	p	b	c	c
w	h	i	c	h

Cut out the letters at the bottom of the page. Then paste them in the correct order to complete the sentence.

_ _ _ _ _ fruit is your favorite?

h W i h c

The e in she
makes a long e sound,
like in bee.

Say the word. Then trace the word.

she she she she

Write the word.

Color each space that has the word she.

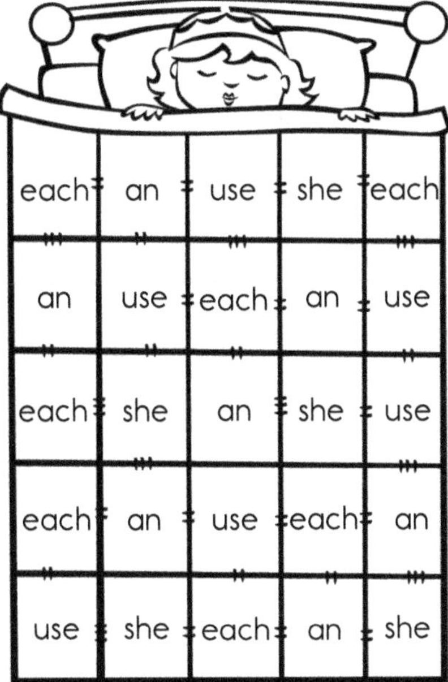

Find the word she. Draw a line to connect the letters.

Cut out the letters at the bottom of the page. Then paste them in the correct order to complete the sentence.

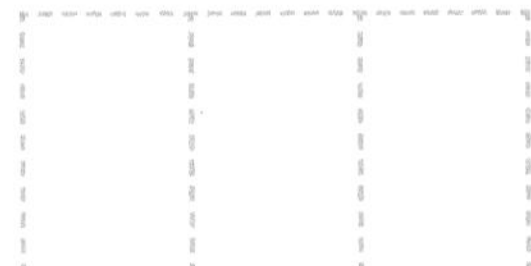 has a camera.

do

Say the word. Then trace the word.

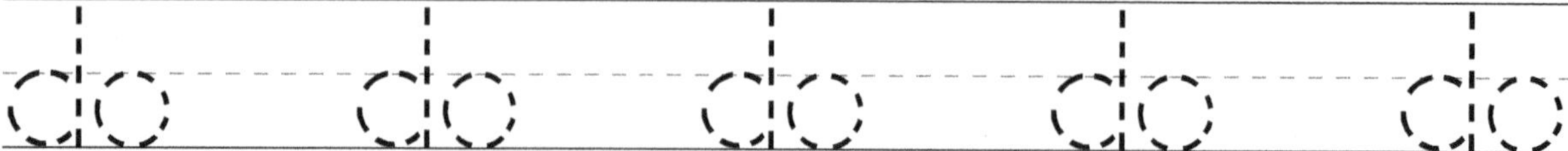

Write the word.

Circle each dolphin that has the word do.

How many times can you find the word do?

do the do do and to the the in do and do of do

☐ times

Cut out the letters at the bottom of the page. Then paste them in the correct order to complete the sentence.

☐☐ you like blueberry muffins?

✂ o D

How rhymes with now and cow.

Say the word. Then trace the word.

how how how how

Write the word.

Circle each plum that has the word how.

Fill in the missing letters to write the word how.

h_ _ _o_

h_w _ow

_ _w ho_

Cut out the letters at the bottom of the page. Then paste them in the correct order to complete the sentence.

_ _ _ do you like my sunglasses?

The word their sounds just like the word there.

Say the word. Then trace the word.

their their their

Write the word.

Begin at the red arrow. Connect the dots to finish the picture.

their

their

their

their

their

their

their

STOP

How many times can you find the word their?

each their how
she an
which their do
their in *which* their
each do their

Cut out the letters at the bottom of the page. Then paste them in the correct order to complete the sentence.

That is ______ house.

h t i r e

The letter i in if makes a short i sound, like in mitt.

Say the word. Then trace the word.

if if if if if

Write the word.

Draw a line to match each word.

IF	if
if	IF
if	if
if	**if**

Find and circle the word if three times.

g	o	d	i	f
t	e	u	x	n
b	h	p	i	l
i	r	z	f	s
y	f	c	q	a

Cut out the letters at the bottom of the page. Then paste them in the correct order to complete the sentence.

[ ][ ] I had a guinea pig, I would call it George.

f I

will

Say the word. Then trace the word.

Write the word.

Color each space that has the word will.

Find the word will. Draw a line to connect the letters.

Cut out the letters at the bottom of the page. Then paste them in the correct order to complete the sentence.

We  go to the movies tonight.

l l i w

The letter u in up makes a short u sound, like in yum.

Say the word. Then trace the word.

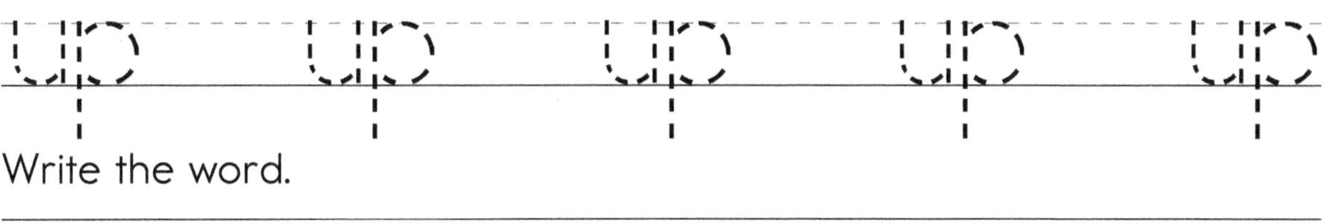

Write the word.

Circle each star that has the word up.

will up

up if

up each

Complete the maze. Color the circles that have the word up.

up	will	if	their	how
up	up	up	up	do
she	will	if	up	up
their	how	do	she	up
will	if	their	how	up

Cut out the letters at the bottom of the page. Then paste them in the correct order to complete the sentence.

The hot air balloon

goes ___ ___ in the sky.

p u

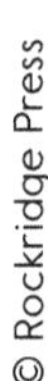

other

Say the word. Then trace the word.

other other other

Write the word.

Color each space that has the word other.

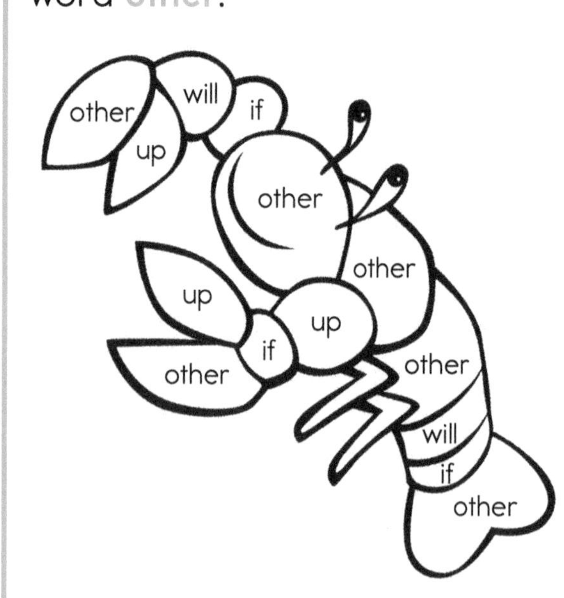

Fill in the missing letters to write the word other.

o _ _ _ r _ _ he _

_ _ _ _ r _ t _ _ _

Cut out the letters at the bottom of the page. Then paste them in the correct order to complete the sentence.

Let's help each _ _ _ _ _

build a castle.

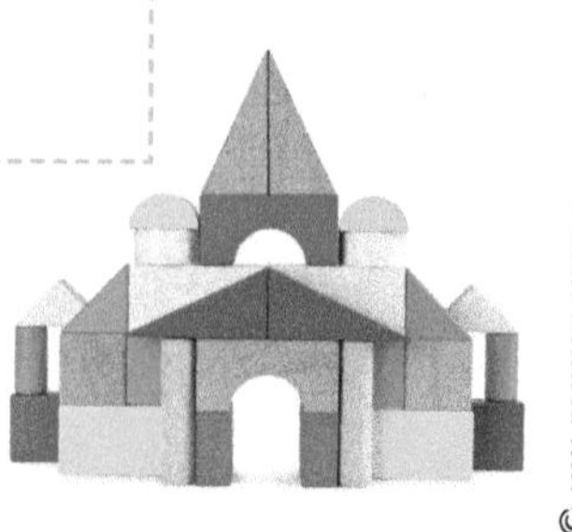

Say the word. Then trace the word.

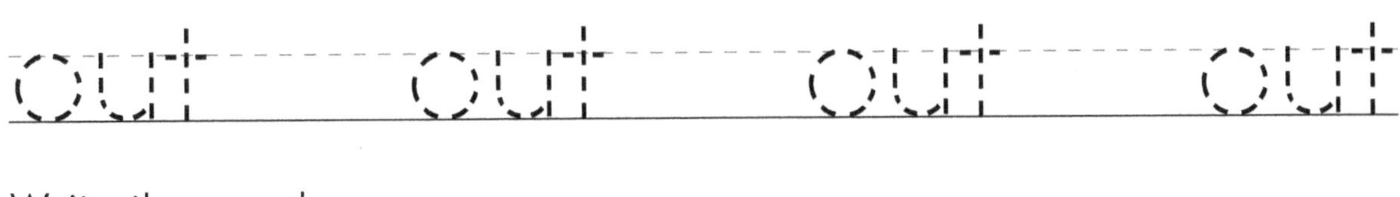

Write the word.

Begin at the red arrow. Connect the dots to finish the picture.

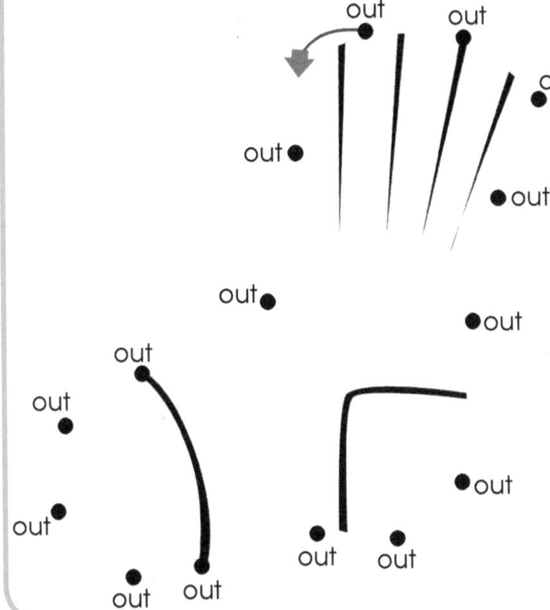

How many times can you find the word out?

out will out
use
other up can
out if out their
will and out

Cut out the letters at the bottom of the page. Then paste them in the correct order to complete the sentence.

Look ☐☐☐ the window.

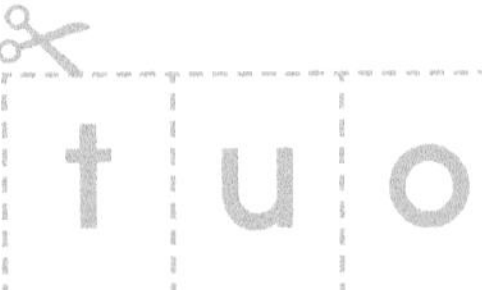

about

Say the word. Then trace the word.

about about about

Write the word.

Draw a line to match each word.	Find and circle the word about three times.
about about ABOUT **about** **about** about about ABOUT	a p a j w r b b w m a b o u t v p u u q y i t n t

Cut out the letters at the bottom of the page. Then paste them in the correct order to complete the sentence.

What is the book

t u o b a

Say the word. Then trace the word.

many many many

Write the word.

Color each space that has the word many.

Find the word many. Draw a line to connect the letters.

Cut out the letters at the bottom of the page. Then paste them in the correct order to complete the sentence.

I saw 

butterflies.

The letter e in then makes a short e sound, like in pet.

Say the word. Then trace the word.

then then then

Write the word.

Begin at the red arrow. Connect the dots to finish the picture.

then then then then then then then then then then then then then

Complete the maze. Color the circles that have the word then.

Cut out the letters at the bottom of the page. Then paste them in the correct order to complete the sentence.

If I finish dinner, ____

I can have dessert.

The word them has a short e sound, like in met.

Say the word. Then trace the word.

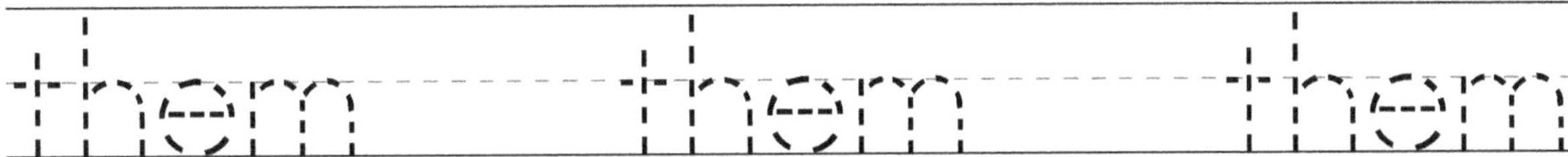

Write the word.

Color each space that has the word them.

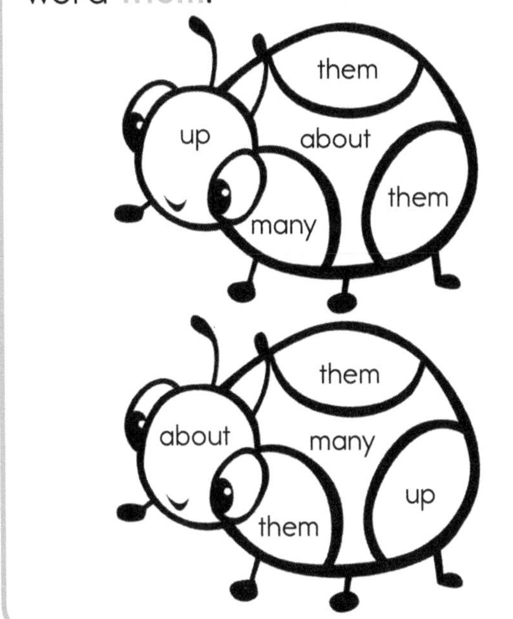

Fill in the missing letters to write the word them.

t___ _h__

t__m __em

___m th__

Cut out the letters at the bottom of the page. Then paste them in the correct order to complete the sentence.

He likes to blow bubbles and pop .

m e h t

these

Say the word. Then trace the word.

these these these

Write the word.

Circle each treasure chest that has the word these.

How many times can you find the word these?

then these
these about
if many up
then these these she
which if these

☐ times

Cut out the letters at the bottom of the page. Then paste them in the correct order to complete the sentence.

☐☐☐☐☐ gummies

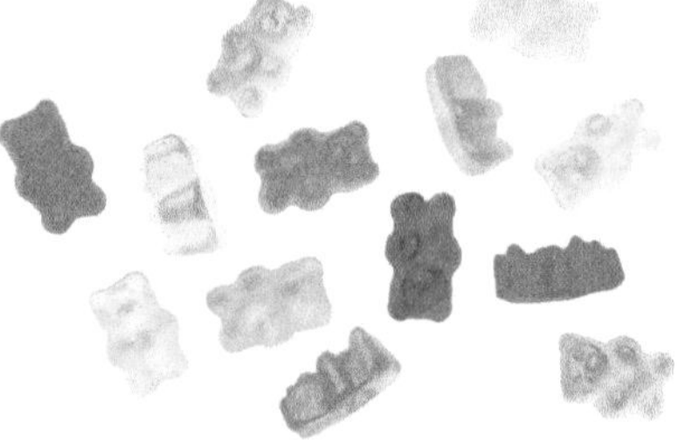

are yummy!

The word so has a long o sound, like in nose.

Say the word. Then trace the word.

so so so so so

Write the word.

Draw a line to match each word.

so so

so so

so so

so so

Find and circle the word so three times.

f p d j w
s e s x n
b o o q l
u r c v t
y i s o a

Cut out the letters at the bottom of the page. Then paste them in the correct order to complete

The playground was [ ] [ ] fun!

o s

some

Say the word. Then trace the word.

some some some

Write the word.

Color each space that has the word some.

Find the word some. Draw a line to connect the letters.

Cut out the letters at the bottom of the page. Then paste them in the correct order to complete the sentence.

Here is  water.

e m o s

Say the word. Then trace the word.

her her her her

Write the word.

Begin at the red arrow. Connect the dots to finish the picture.

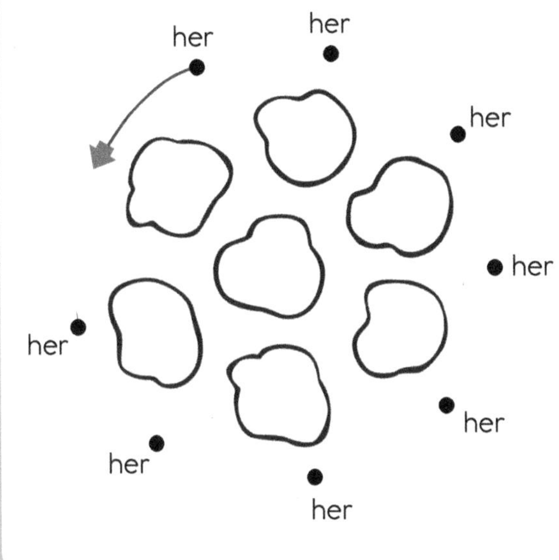

Complete the maze. Color the circles that have the word her.

Cut out the letters at the bottom of the page. Then paste them in the correct order to complete the sentence.

hair is brown.

would

Say the word. Then trace the word.

would would would

Write the word.

Color each space that has the word would.

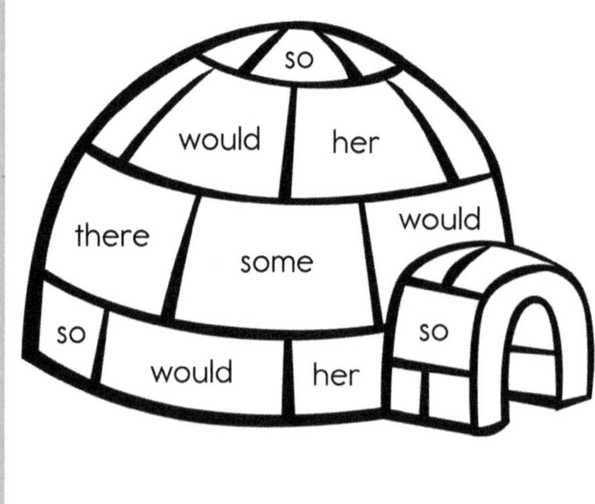

Fill in the missing letters to write the word would.

w____ __u__

w___d __ul_

____d _o___

Cut out the letters at the bottom of the page. Then paste them in the correct order to complete the sentence.

I _____ like a banana.

d l w o u

Say the word. Then trace the word.

make make make

Write the word.

Circle each top that has the word make.

How many times can you find the word make?

her make some make make to the these them would make make of so

Cut out the letters at the bottom of the page. Then paste them in the correct order to complete the sentence.

Let's

cupcakes!

like

The i in like sounds the same as the y in try.

Say the word. Then trace the word.

like like like like

Write the word.

Draw a line to match each word.

LIKE	like
like	LIKE
like	**like**
like	like

Find and circle the word like three times.

f	l	d	h	w
l	e	i	x	n
i	g	p	k	m
k	l	i	k	e
e	j	c	q	y

Cut out the letters at the bottom of the page. Then paste them in the correct order to complete the sentence.

I ☐☐☐☐ to draw.

i	l	e	k

Say the word. Then trace the word.

Write the word.

Color each space that has the word two.

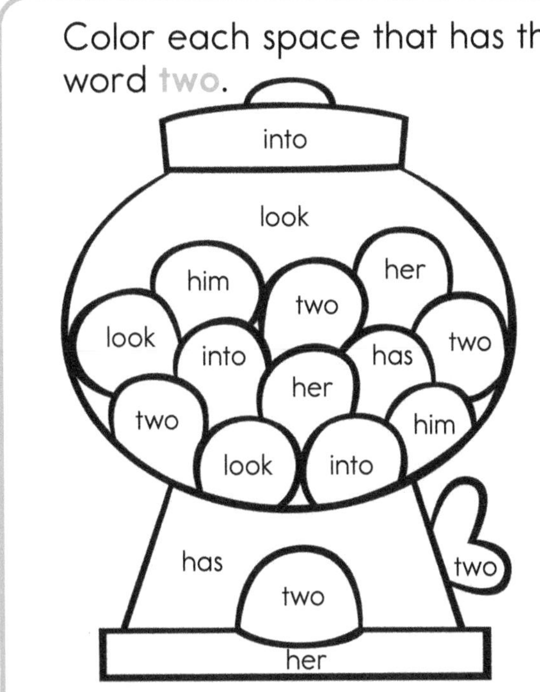

Find the word two. Draw a line to connect the letters.

Cut out the letters at the bottom of the page. Then paste them in the correct order to complete the sentence.

I have 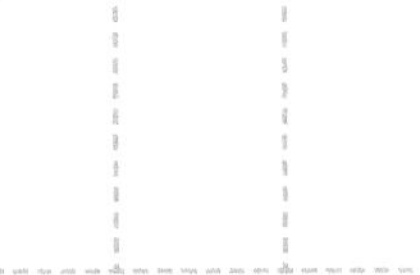 shells.

w o t

more

Say the word. Then trace the word.

more more more

Write the word.

Begin at the red arrow. Connect the dots to finish the picture.

Complete the maze. Color the circles that have the word more.

more	more	two	look	has
time	more	into	him	like
make	more	time	look	has
two	more	make	time	him
has	more	more	more	more

Cut out the letters at the bottom of the page. Then paste them in the correct order to complete the sentence.

May I have 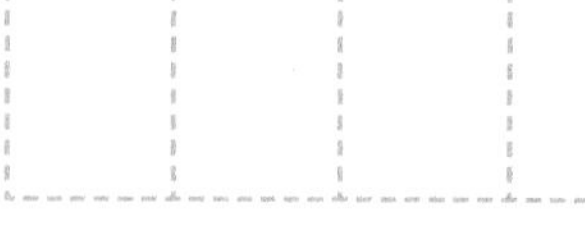 spaghetti?

r o e m

Say the word. Then trace the word.

him him him him

Write the word.

Color each space that has the word him.

Find the word him. Draw a line to connect the letters.

Cut out the letters at the bottom of the page. Then paste them in the correct order to complete the sentence.

She is playing with ___ ___ ___.

If you can read the words in and to, then put them together and you can read into.

Say the word. Then trace the word.

into into into into

Write the word.

Begin at the red arrow. Connect the dots to finish the picture.

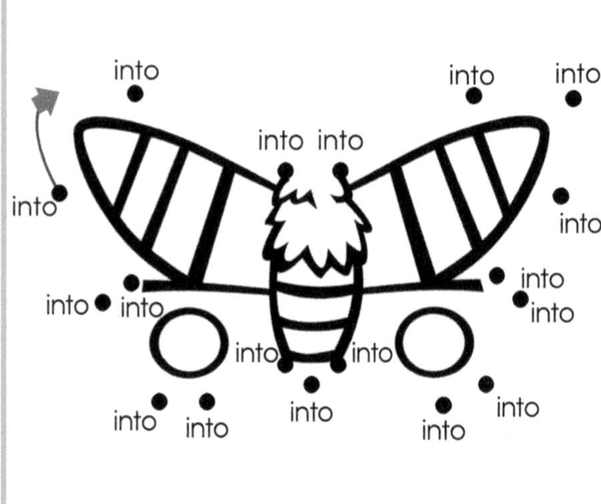

Complete the maze. Color the circles that have the word into.

Cut out the letters at the bottom of the page. Then paste them in the correct order to complete the sentence.

Put the cookie

☐☐☐☐ the jar.

i t o n

The e in time is silent.

Say the word. Then trace the word.

time time time time

Write the word.

Color each space that has the word time.

Fill in the missing letters to write the word time.

t_ _e _ _me

_ _ _e ti_ _

Cut out the letters at the bottom of the page. Then paste them in the correct order to complete the sentence.

What is it?

m e i t

has

Say the word. Then trace the word.

has has has has

Write the word.

Circle each clam that has the word has.

How many times can you find the word has?

has has him
make
time like has
has into her would
has him has

 times

Cut out the letters at the bottom of the page. Then paste them in the correct order to complete the sentence.

He  a guitar.

s a h

Say the word. Then trace the word.

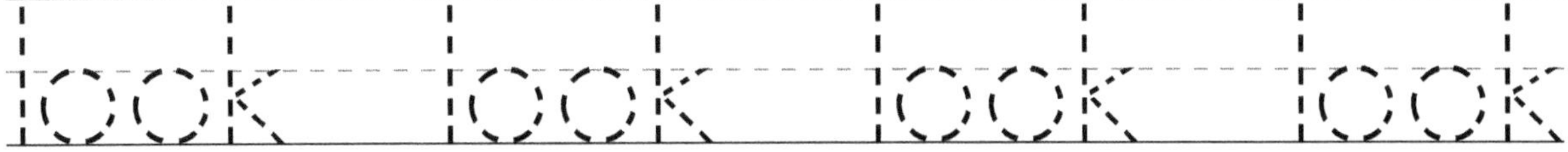

Write the word.

Draw a line to match each word.

look	**look**
LOOK	look
look	LOOK
look	look

Find and circle the word look three times.

l	m	b	l	x
t	o	u	o	n
d	g	o	o	m
l	o	o	k	s
w	i	b	p	y

Cut out the letters at the bottom of the page. Then paste them in the correct order to complete the sentence.

_ _ _ _ what she can do!

o o L k

Say the word. Then trace the word.

write write write

Write the word.

Color each space that has the word write.

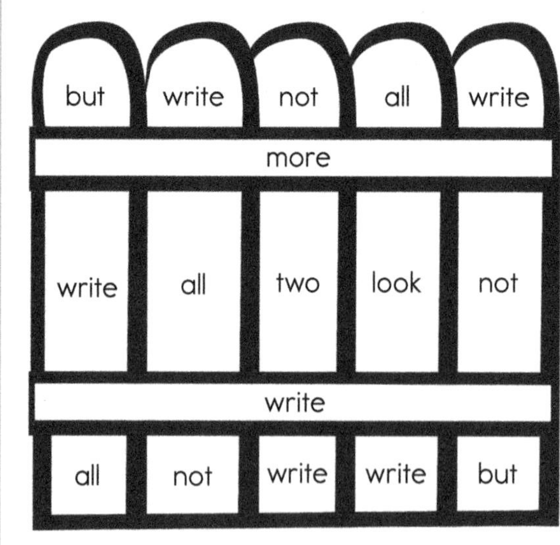

Fill in the missing letters to write the word write.

w_ _ _ _ _ _ i _ _

w_ _ _ e _ _ i t _

_ _ _ _ e _ r _ _ _

Cut out the letters at the bottom of the page. Then paste them in the correct order to complete the sentence.

I can _____ my name.

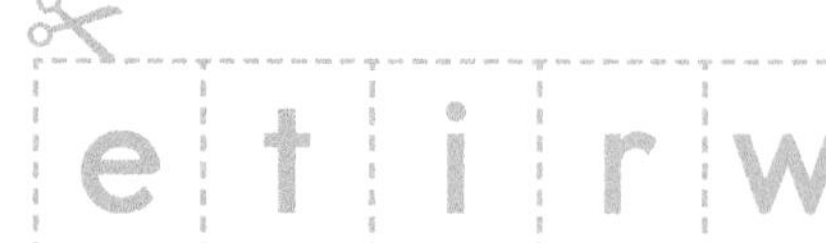

The word go has a long o sound, just like the word so.

Say the word. Then trace the word.

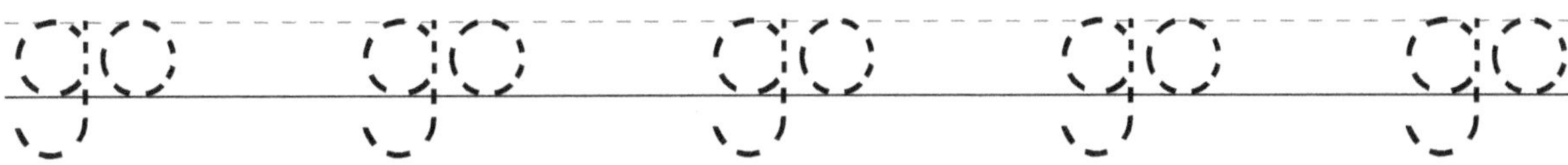

Write the word.

Circle each teacup that has the word go.

How many times can you find the word go?

go go to go and to the the in the and the of go

Cut out the letters at the bottom of the page. Then paste them in the correct order to complete the sentence.

When can we  on a plane?

see

The ee in see sounds like the long e in he.

Say the word. Then trace the word.

see see see see

Write the word.

Draw a line to match each word.

SEE	see
see	SEE
see	**see**
see	see

Find and circle the word see three times.

s	o	d	j	w
y	e	s	e	e
b	g	e	q	l
u	p	e	v	t
x	i	c	n	a

Cut out the letters at the bottom of the page. Then paste them in the correct order to complete the sentence.

I ☐☐☐

three sweet treats.

e s e

number

Say the word. Then trace the word.

Write the word.

Color each space that has the word number.

number
see
go
number
write
see
write
number
go
number

Find the word number. Draw a line to connect the letters.

Cut out the letters at the bottom of the page. Then paste them in the correct order to complete the sentence.

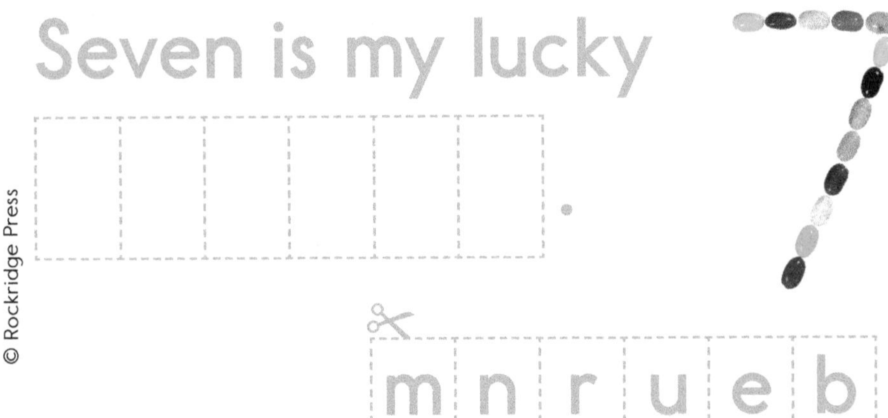

no

No rhymes with so and go.

Say the word. Then trace the word.

no no no no no

Write the word.

Begin at the red arrow. Connect the dots to finish the picture.

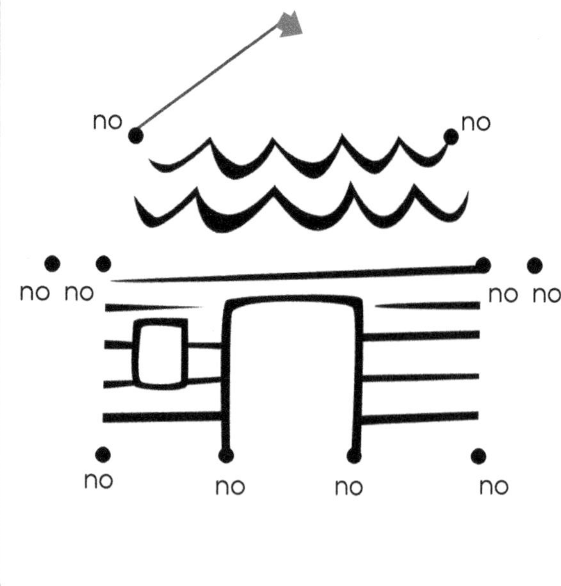

Complete the maze. Color the circles that have the word no.

Cut out the letters at the bottom of the page. Then paste them in the correct order to complete the sentence.

[ ][ ] thanks. I don't want a sandwich.

o N

Say the word. Then trace the word.

way way way way

Write the word.

Color each space that has the word way.

Fill in the missing letters to write the word way.

w_ _ _a_

w_y _ _y

_ay wa_

Cut out the letters at the bottom of the page. Then paste them in the correct order to complete the sentence.

Go this  ?

a y w

could

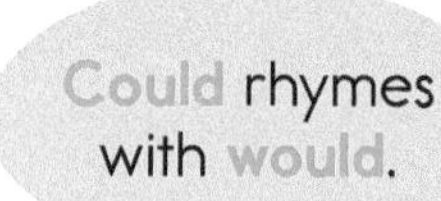

Say the word. Then trace the word.

Write the word.

Circle each gift that has the word could.

How many times can you find the word could?

could
words no you
could could way
into would has
could
could way could

times

Cut out the letters at the bottom of the page. Then paste them in the correct order to complete the sentence.

I ☐☐☐☐☐ play

with this kitten all day.

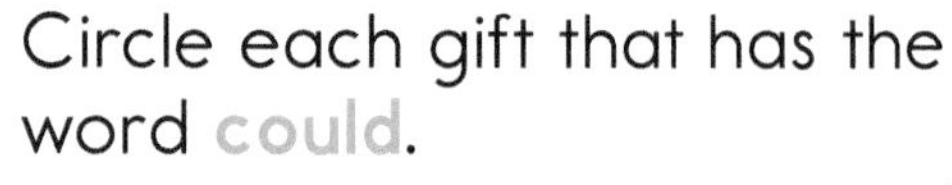

Say the word. Then trace the word.

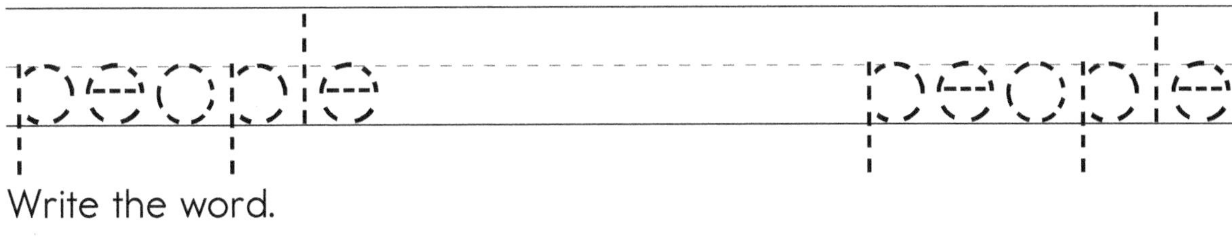

Write the word.

Draw a line to match each word.

people	people
people	PEOPLE
people	**people**
PEOPLE	people

Find and circle the word people three times.

p	p	d	s	g	f
p	e	o	p	l	e
j	o	o	t	w	m
v	p	f	p	r	k
z	l	o	a	l	r
c	e	i	b	a	e

Cut out the letters at the bottom of the page. Then paste them in the correct order to complete the sentence.

Many ☐☐☐☐☐☐ ride the bus.

l	e	p	o	e	p

The y in my makes a long i sound, as in bike.

Say the word. Then trace the word.

my my my my my

Write the word.

Color each space that has the word my.

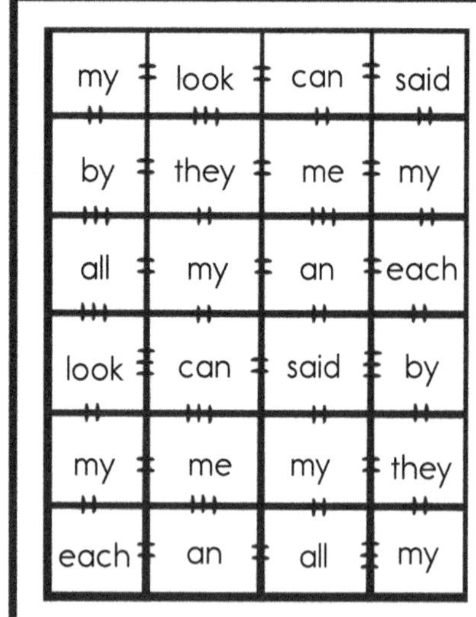

my	look	can	said
by	they	me	my
all	my	an	each
look	can	said	by
my	me	my	they
each	an	all	my

Find the word my. Draw a line to connect the letters.

Cut out the letters at the bottom of the page. Then paste them in the correct order to complete the sentence.

This is ☐☐ new shirt.

y m

Than has a short a sound. What other words have a short a sound?

Say the word. Then trace the word.

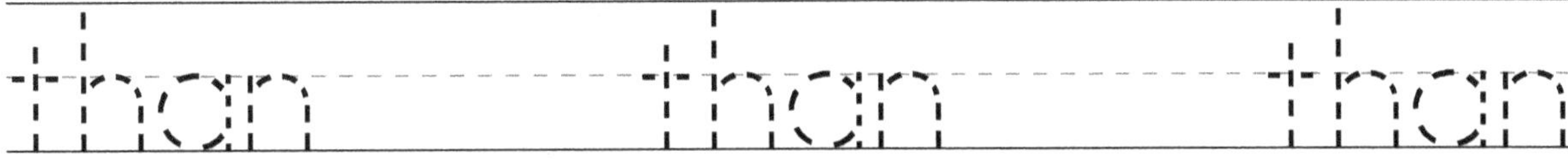

Write the word.

Begin at the red arrow. Connect the dots to finish the picture.

than

than

than

than

than

than

than

Complete the maze. Color the circles that have the word than.

than	my	way	no	see
than	than	than	he	if
we	if	than	than	see
he	my	way	than	than
no	see	is	he	than

Cut out the letters at the bottom of the page. Then paste them in the correct order to complete the sentence.

She is taller ____ her brother.

n h a t

Say the word. Then trace the word.

first first first first

Write the word.

Color each space that has the word first.

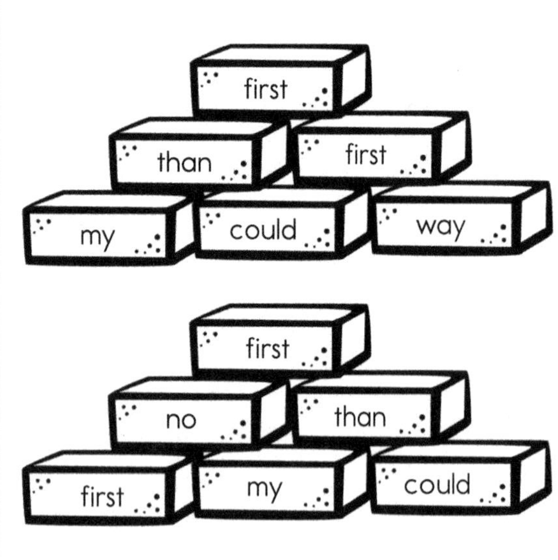

Fill in the missing letters to write the word first.

f _ _ _ _   _ _ r _ _

f _ _ _ t   _ _ r s _

_ _ _ _ t   _ i _ _ _

Cut out the letters at the bottom of the page. Then paste them in the correct order to complete the sentence.

Which one is

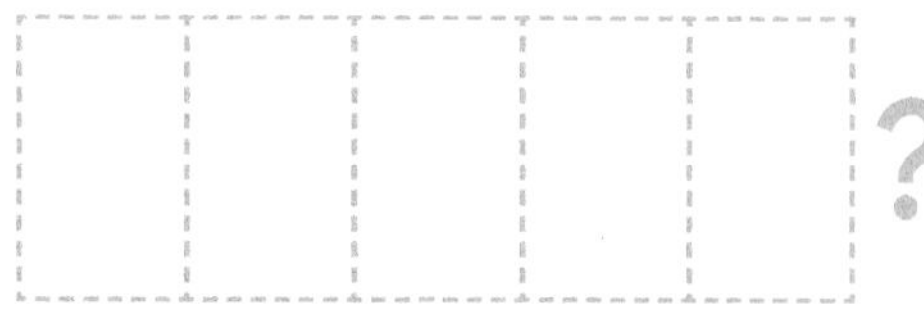

?

t i r f s

Say the word. Then trace the word.

water water water

Write the word.

Circle each cup that has the word water.

How many times can you find the word water?

water my than
for first
people water the
people
water for could
than water water

☐ times

Cut out the letters at the bottom of the page. Then paste them in the correct order to complete the sentence.

Are you ready to go

in the ☐☐☐☐☐?

r w a e t

been

Say the word. Then trace the word.

been been been

Write the word.

Draw a line to match each word.		Find and circle the word been three times.
been	been	b e e n v
BEEN	been	s e b w m
been	been	c f e p k
been	BEEN	t o e n r
		x h n o z

Cut out the letters at the bottom of the page. Then paste them in the correct order to complete the sentence.

Have you ever 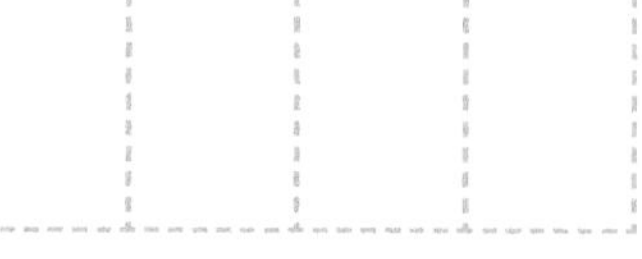

on a sailboat?

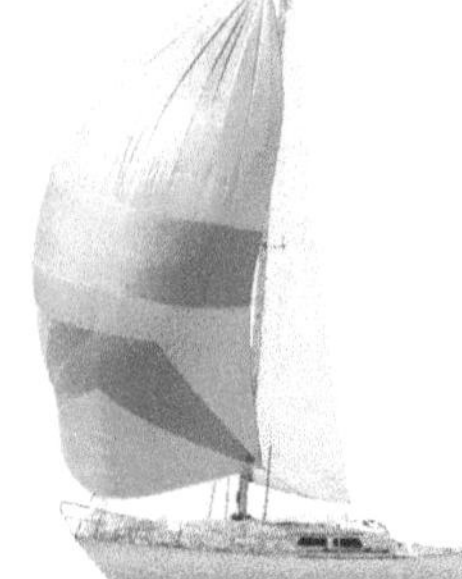

Say the word. Then trace the word.

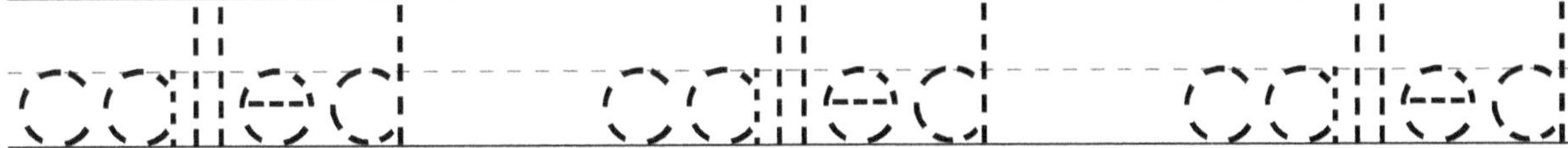

Write the word.

Color each space that has the word called.

Find the word called. Draw a line to connect the letters.

Cut out the letters at the bottom of the page. Then paste them in the correct order to complete the sentence.

I ______ my

grandma today.

l c a d l e

who

The sounds h and oo make the word who.

Say the word. Then trace the word.

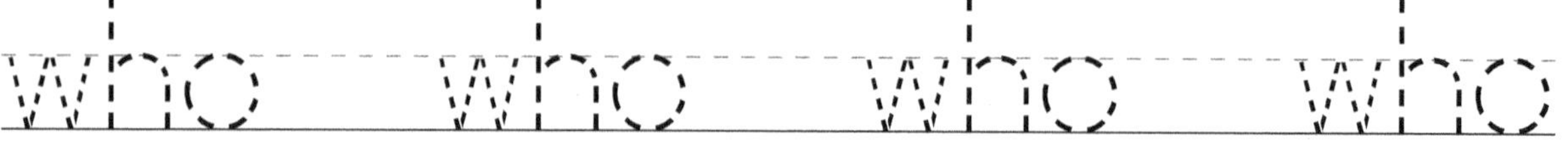

Write the word.

Begin at the red arrow. Connect the dots to finish the picture.

Complete the maze. Color the circles that have the word who.

Cut out the letters at the bottom of the page. Then paste them in the correct order to complete the sentence.

wants to come to my party?

o h W

Two sounds make the word am: short a and m.

Say the word. Then trace the word.

am am am am am

Write the word.

Color each space that has the word am.

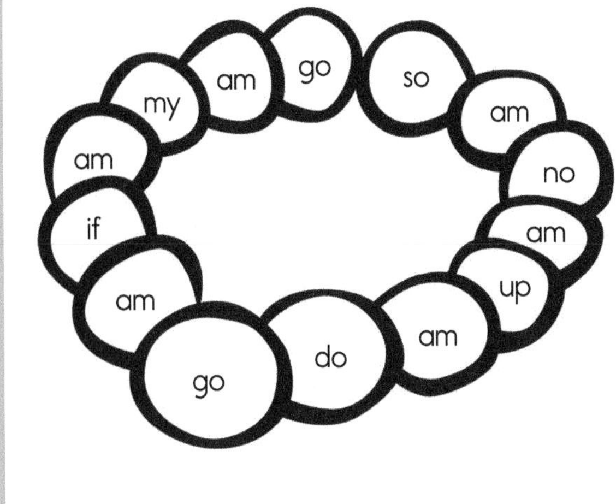

How many times can you find the word am?

who am am am called who than first am water am been am

Cut out the letters at the bottom of the page. Then paste them in the correct order to complete the sentence.

I ___ ___ a superhero!

its

Say the word. Then trace the word.

its its its its its

Write the word.

Circle each mitten that has the word its.

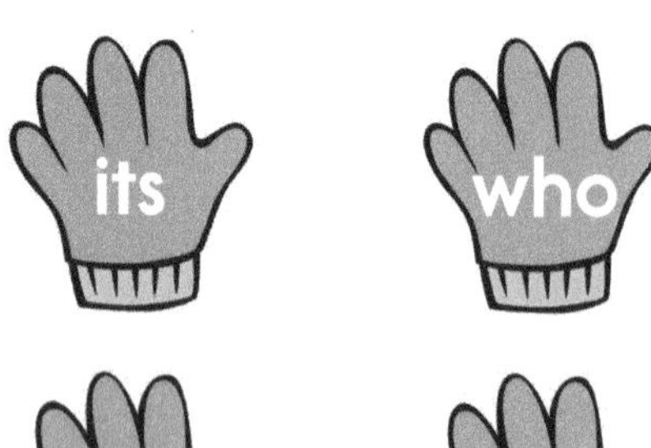

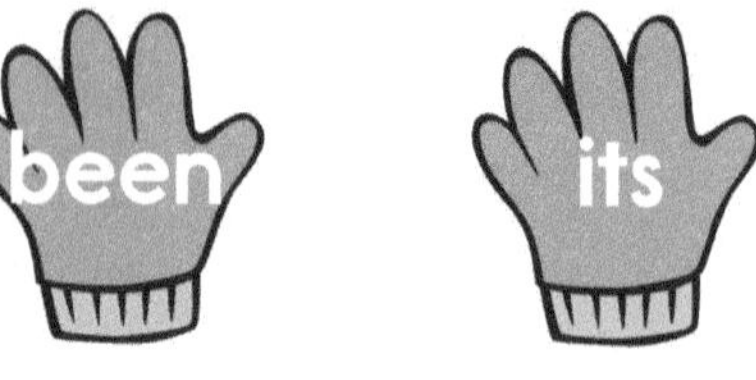

Fill in the missing letters to write the word its.

i _ _   _ t _

i _ s   _ t s

_ _ s   i t _

Cut out the letters at the bottom of the page. Then paste them in the correct order to complete the sentence.

See the koala? 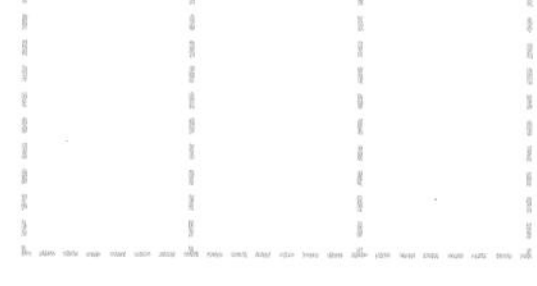

nose is black.

t s I

Say the word. Then trace the word.

now now now now

Write the word.

Draw a line to match each word.

now	now
now	NOW
now	**now**
NOW	now

Find and circle the word now three times.

f	n	d	h	u
t	o	n	x	n
c	w	s	o	o
t	p	a	v	w
z	i	c	m	y

Cut out the letters at the bottom of the page. Then paste them in the correct order to complete the sentence.

What time

is it  ?

The word find has a long i sound, like in time.

Say the word. Then trace the word.

find find find find

Write the word.

Color each space that has the word find.

Find the word find. Draw a line to connect the letters.

Cut out the letters at the bottom of the page. Then paste them in the correct order to complete the sentence.

Let's

some treasure!

d i n f

Long rhymes with strong.

Say the word. Then trace the word.

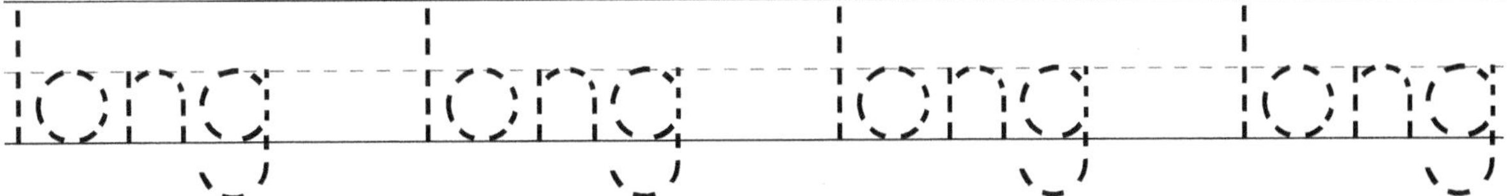

Write the word.

Begin at the red arrow. Connect the dots to finish the picture.

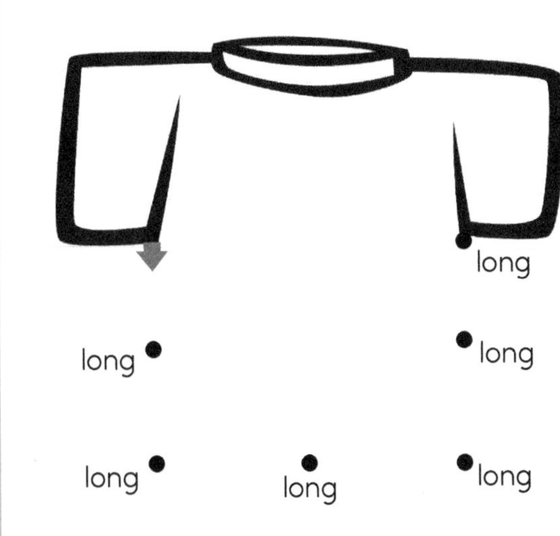

Complete the maze. Color the circles that have the word long.

Cut out the letters at the bottom of the page. Then paste them in the correct order to complete the sentence.

A giraffe has a ______ neck.

n o l g

down

Say the word. Then trace the word.

down down down

Write the word.

Color each space that has the word down.

Fill in the missing letters to write the word down.

d___ _o__

d__n __wn

___n do__

Cut out the letters at the bottom of the page. Then paste them in the correct order to complete the sentence.

We go 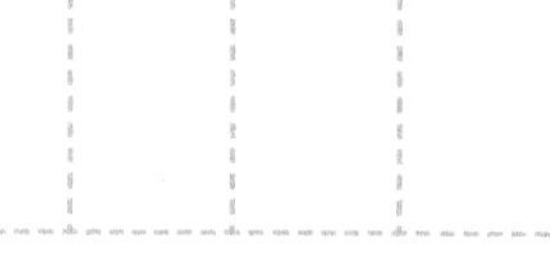

the hill!

The word day has three letters, but only two sounds: d – ay

Say the word. Then trace the word.

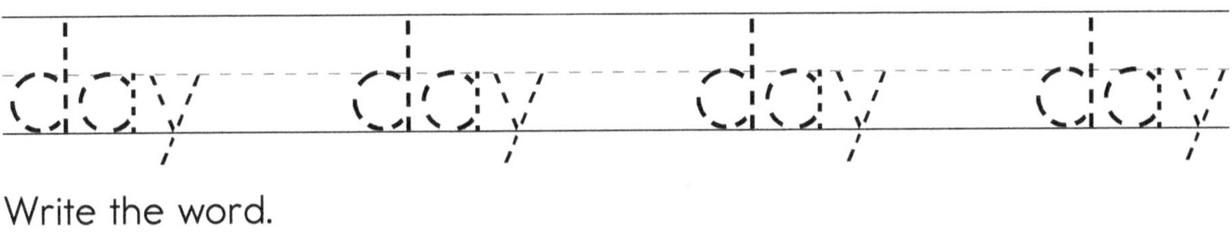

Write the word.

Circle each candy that has the word day.

How many times can you find the word day?

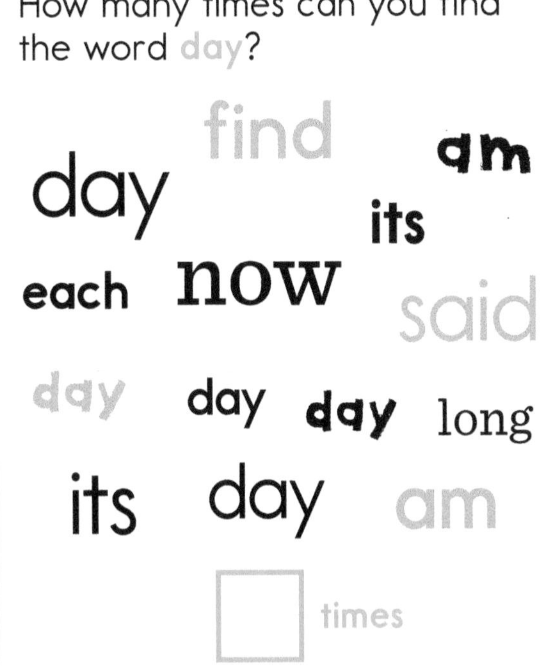

Cut out the letters at the bottom of the page. Then paste them in the correct order to complete the sentence.

We play during the 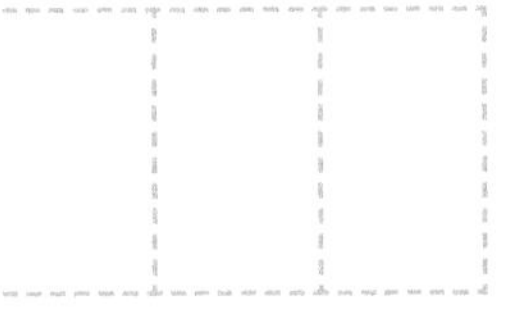

and sleep at night.

did

The word did has a short i sound, like in it.

Say the word. Then trace the word.

did did did did

Write the word.

Draw a line to match each word.

did	
did	did
	did
did	**did**

Find and circle the word did three times.

d	i	d	g	w
t	e	u	i	n
b	h	p	q	d
s	m	b	v	i
y	j	c	k	d

Cut out the letters at the bottom of the page. Then paste them in the correct order to complete the sentence.

[ ][ ][ ] you go to school today?

d D i

Get rhymes with met and wet.

Say the word. Then trace the word.

Write the word.

Color each space that has the word get.

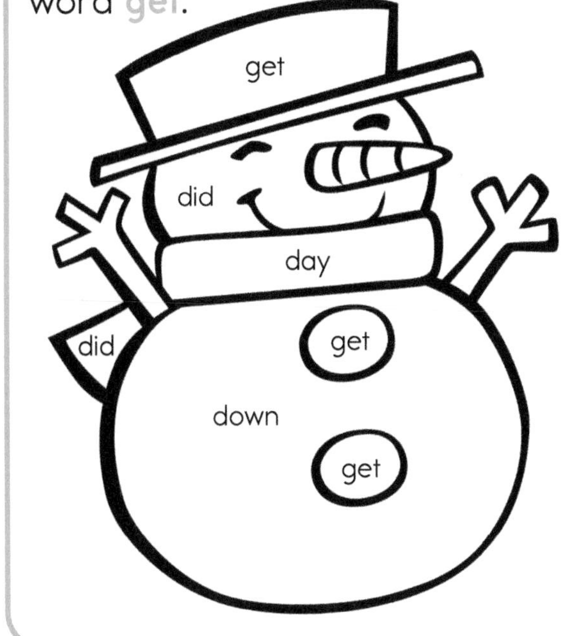

Find the word get. Draw a line to connect the letters.

Cut out the letters at the bottom of the page. Then paste them in the correct order to complete the sentence.

Will you ___ me a snack, please?

come

Say the word. Then trace the word.

come come come

Write the word.

Begin at the red arrow. Connect the dots to finish the picture.

Complete the maze. Color the circles that have the word come.

Cut out the letters at the bottom of the page. Then paste them in the correct order to complete the sentence.

Want to [ ] [ ] [ ] [ ]

over and play?

Say the word. Then trace the word.

made made made

Write the word.

Color each space that has the word made.

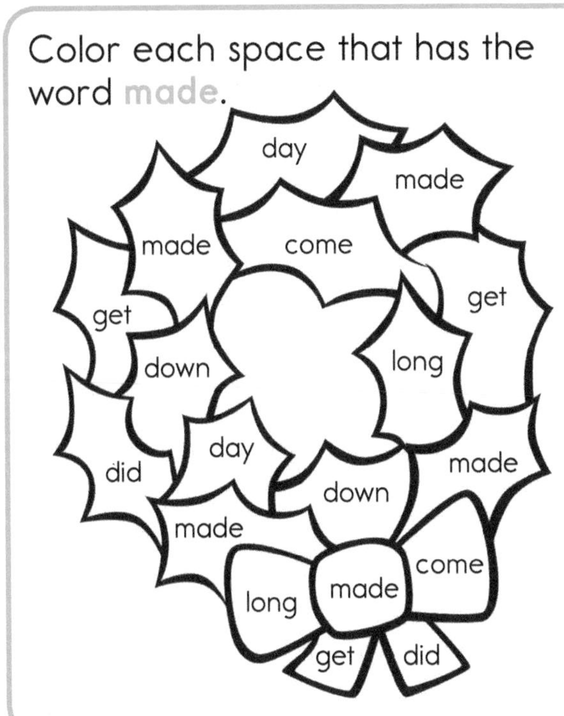

Fill in the missing letters to write the word made.

m___ _a__

m__e __de

___e ma__

Cut out the letters at the bottom of the page. Then paste them in the correct order to complete the sentence.

I ☐☐☐☐ a necklace.

d m a e

Say the word. Then trace the word.

may may may may

Write the word.

Circle each star that has the word may.

may may
made come
get may

How many times can you find the word may?

made may
day do get
may about about
come may and
may may did

times

Cut out the letters at the bottom of the page. Then paste them in the correct order to complete the sentence.

I go on the swings?

y M a

Say the word. Then trace the word.

part part part

Write the word.

Draw a line to match each word.		Find and circle the word part three times.
part	part	f p a r t
PART	part	p e a x n
part	part	a g p r l
part	PART	r d b u t
		t i c m y

Cut out the letters at the bottom of the page. Then paste them in the correct order to complete the sentence.

A leaf is 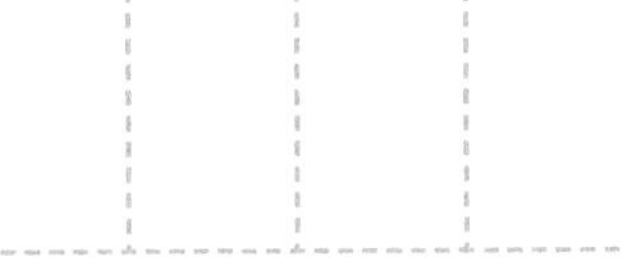

of a flower.

t r p a

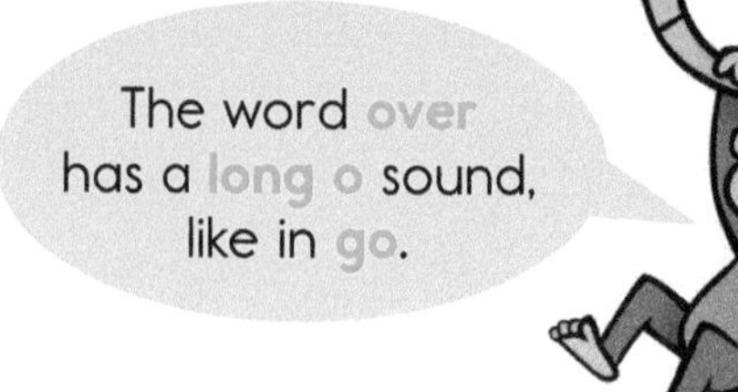

Say the word. Then trace the word.

over over over over

Write the word.

Color each space that has the word over.

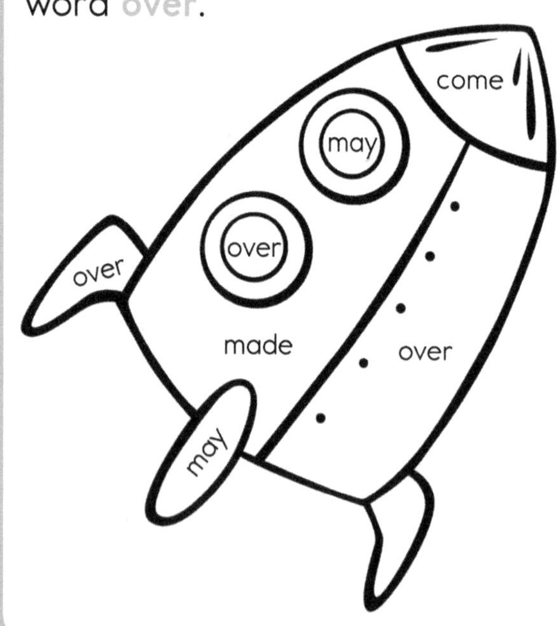

Find the word over. Draw a line to connect the letters.

Cut out the letters at the bottom of the page. Then paste them in the correct order to complete the sentence.

r v e o

BONUS GAME SECTION!

Oink, Oink!

Can you guess what this pig likes to do? Use the key code to find out.

A	E	G	H	I	K
L	O	P	S	T	Y

Butterfly Search

Can you find all the sight words in the puzzle below?

b	h	t	q	y	l	c	a	n
x	f	g	h	p	c	i	w	m
n	o	t	a	e	s	z	e	p
r	c	w	p	l	a	n	r	o
p	m	u	o	v	i	p	e	w
w	i	t	h	r	d	h	m	h
d	j	a	z	p	d	p	f	e
t	h	e	r	e	z	s	u	n

Word Bank

the	can	said
with	when	there
were	not	words

Amazing Amy

Where was Amy? Use the key code to find out.

3 . . . 2 . . . 1 . . . Blast Off!

The sight word rockets need your help!
Color a line from each rocket to the matching star.

Color by Sight Words

Color each square using the color key,
and see what you create using sight words!

as, all, an, he	do, if, out, my	go, did, day, get
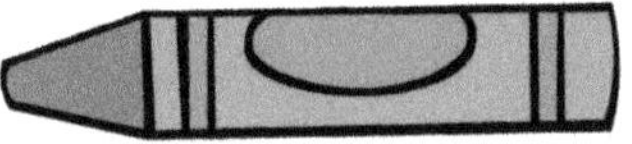	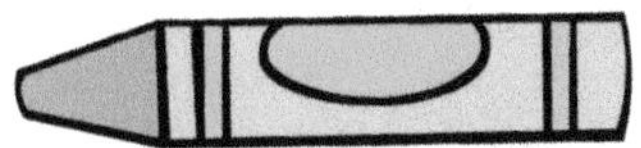	

go	did	day	get	go	did	day	get	go
did	day	as	go	get	day	as	go	did
day	get	an	all	he	all	an	day	get
go	did	do	if	an	out	my	go	did
day	get	out	my	all	do	if	day	get
go	did	an	all	as	all	an	go	did
day	get	do	if	he	out	my	day	get
go	did	out	my	an	do	if	go	did
did	day	get	go	did	day	get	day	get

Hidden Picture

Can you guess what is hidden in the picture? Color the spaces to see!

long = green	**said = red**	**called = purple**
these = blue	**one = orange**	**we = yellow**

Dino Search

Can you find all the sight words in the puzzle below?

b	z	h	l	r	q	w	h	o
t	h	e	y	h	r	o	z	x
n	q	k	m	i	l	u	v	p
u	t	e	b	z	w	l	a	e
m	c	a	l	l	e	d	i	o
b	v	c	u	i	y	w	n	p
e	d	h	p	k	l	a	t	l
r	c	f	r	e	g	z	o	e

Word Bank

he	into
they	number
each	people
would	called
like	who

Honey Buzz

Color a line from each bee to the matching hive.

over

than

now

over

than

now

Sea of Sight Words

Can you find and circle the sight words in the picture?

Word Bank					
find	write	day	time	use	into

Sight Word Fun

Use the color key to color a special friend.

see = pink	**water = green**	**who = purple**
first = blue	**her = brown**	**now = yellow**

Dolphin Search

Can you find all the sight words in the puzzle below?

v	b	t	x	t	b	n	o	w
w	h	d	i	p	u	e	v	k
q	e	u	o	m	a	d	e	x
m	s	g	k	a	e	b	r	n
c	z	w	i	y	r	t	u	o
p	a	r	t	m	k	h	f	s
x	v	n	s	f	i	r	s	t
j	w	a	t	e	r	r	g	z

Word Bank

time	its
part	now
made	first
over	been
may	water

Solve the Puzzle

Use the word bank and the clues to complete the crossword puzzle.

Word Bank

look number long
people time she

1
2 t
3 p
4 n m
5 l k
6 s

1. ____ is the opposite of short.
2. What ____ is the movie?
3. Lots of ______ ride the bus.
4. Three is the ______ after two.
5. We use our eyes to ____ at things.
6. ___ is my friend.

Summer Sight Words

Color each space using the color key.

have = red **what = blue** **all = pink**

each = orange **time = green** **down = yellow**

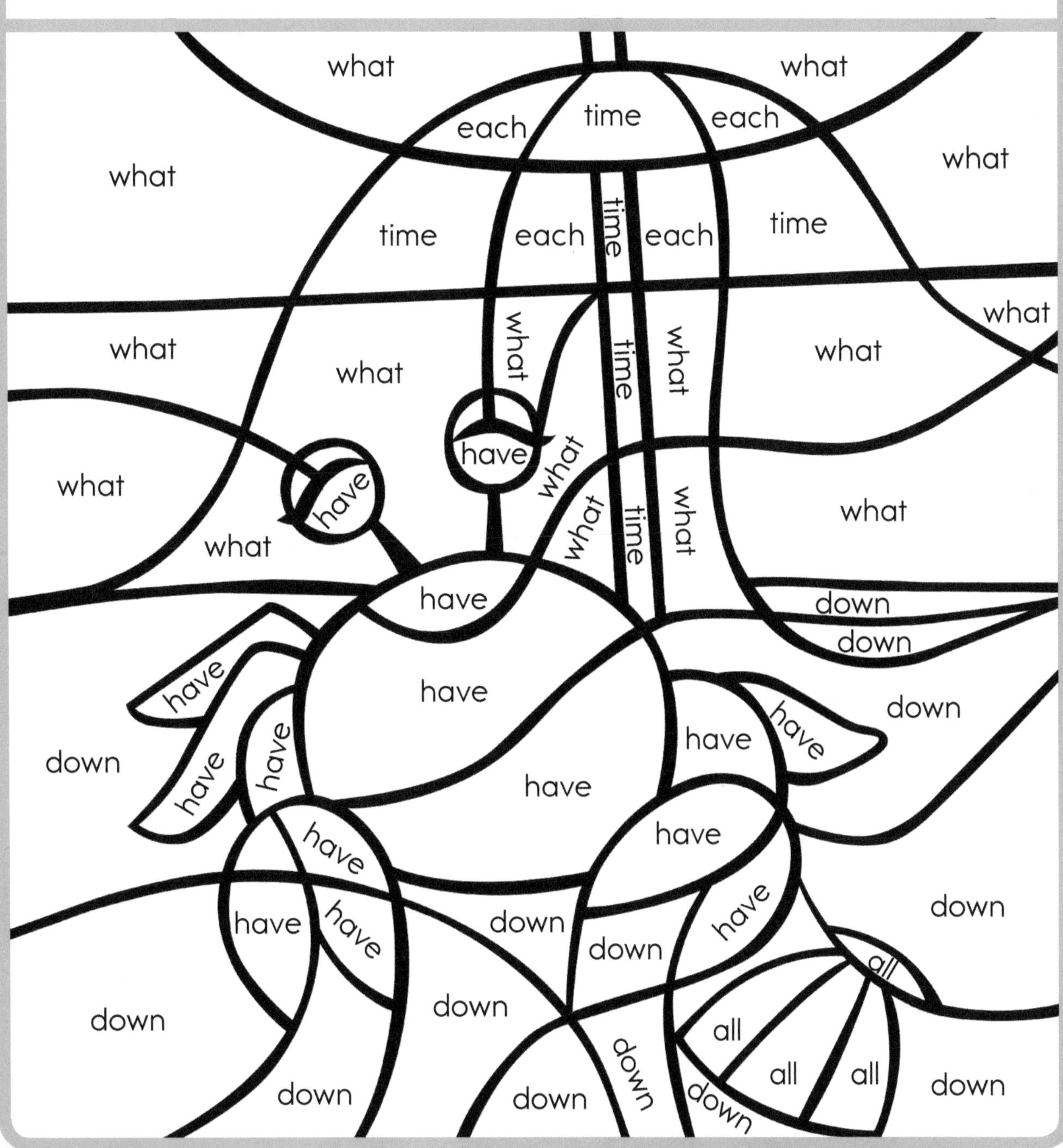

Answer Key

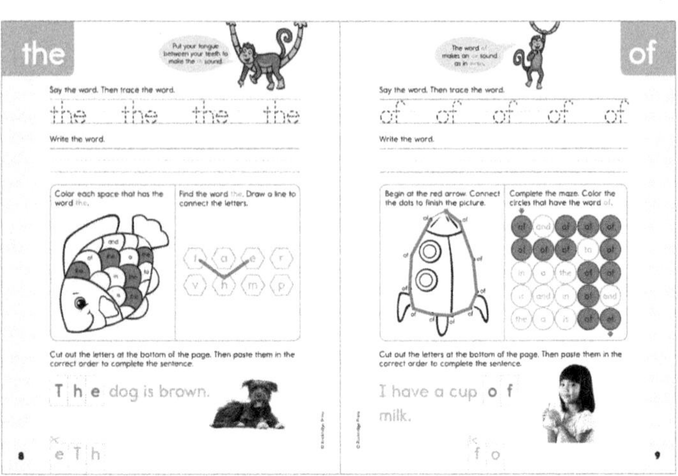

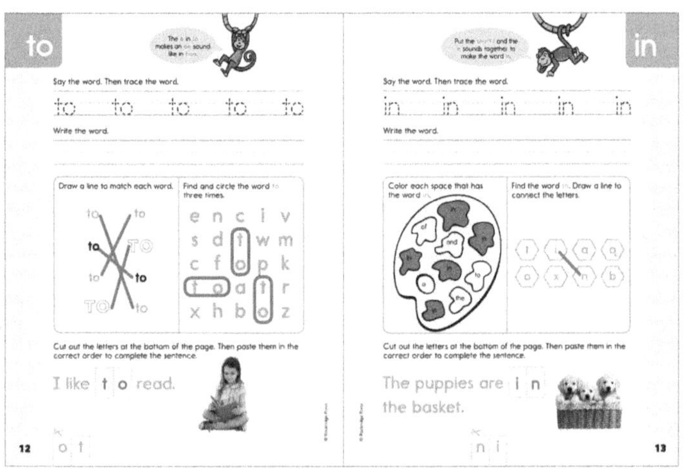

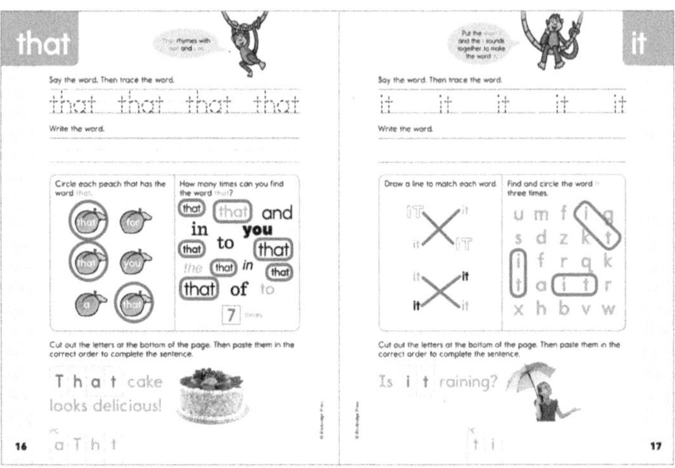

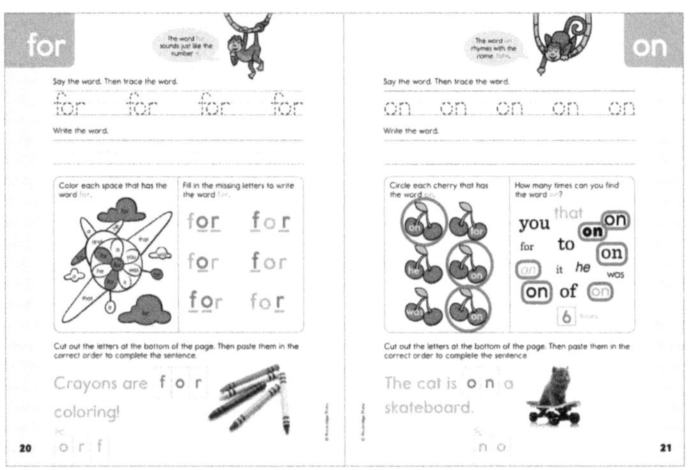
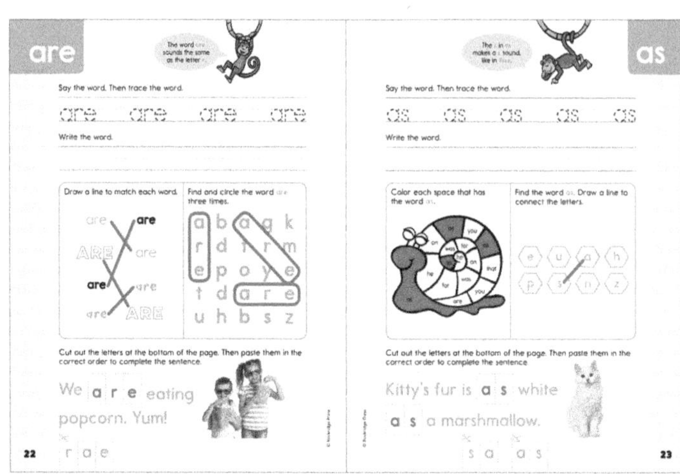
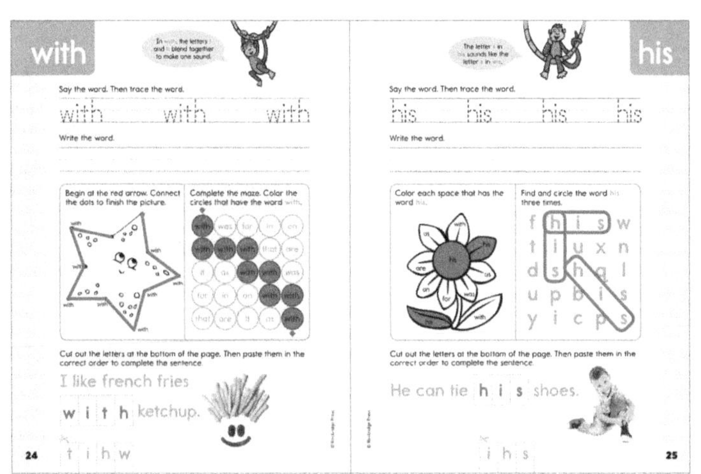

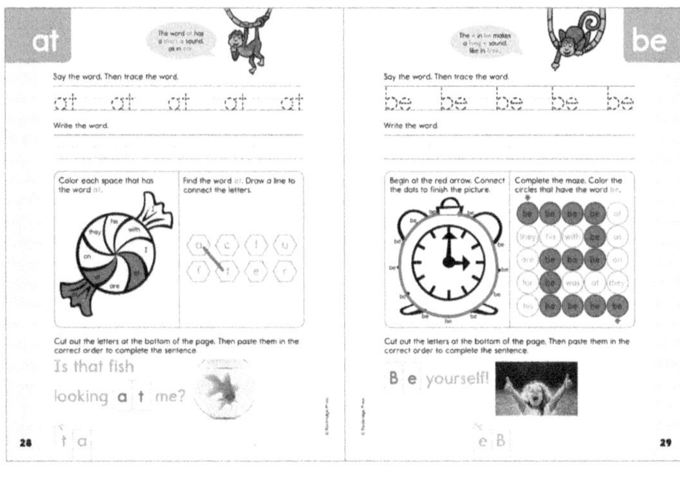

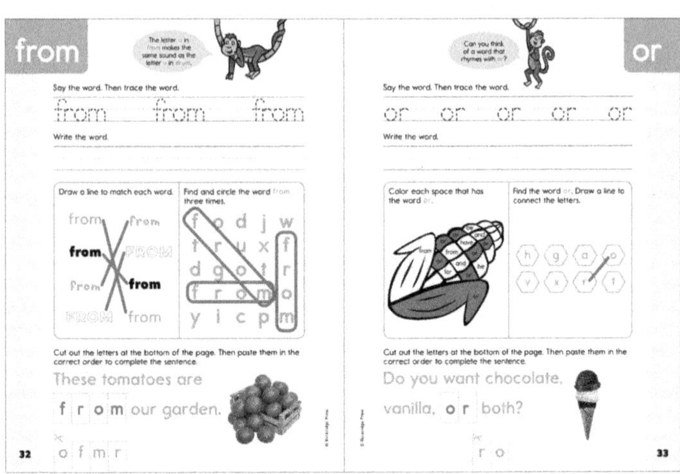
from

Say the word. Then trace the word.

from from from

Write the word.

Draw a line to match each word.

Find and circle the word from three times.

Cut out the letters at the bottom of the page. Then paste them in the correct order to complete the sentence.

These tomatoes are f r o m our garden.

o f m r

32

or

Say the word. Then trace the word.

or or or or or

Write the word.

Color each space that has the word or.

Find the word or. Draw a line to connect the letters.

Cut out the letters at the bottom of the page. Then paste them in the correct order to complete the sentence.

Do you want chocolate, vanilla, o r both?

r o

33

one

Say the word. Then trace the word.

one one one one

Write the word.

Begin at the red arrow. Connect the dots to finish the picture.

Complete the maze. Color the circles that have the word one.

Cut out the letters at the bottom of the page. Then paste them in the correct order to complete the sentence.

I have o n e special teddy bear.

e o n

34

had

Say the word. Then trace the word.

had had had had

Write the word.

Color each space that has the word had.

Fill in the missing letters to write the word had.

had had had had had had

Cut out the letters at the bottom of the page. Then paste them in the correct order to complete the sentence.

We h a d fun at the beach.

d a h

35

by

Say the word. Then trace the word.

by by by by by

Write the word.

Circle each heart that has the word by.

How many times can you find the word by?

4 times

Cut out the letters at the bottom of the page. Then paste them in the correct order to complete the sentence.

I can do this all b y myself!

y b

36

words

Say the word. Then trace the word.

words words words

Write the word.

Draw a line to match each word.

Find and circle the word words three times.

Cut out the letters at the bottom of the page. Then paste them in the correct order to complete the sentence.

I can write lots of w o r d s.

r o d s w

37

but

Say the word. Then trace the word.

but but but but

Write the word.

Color each space that has the word but.

Find the word but. Draw a line to connect the letters.

Cut out the letters at the bottom of the page. Then paste them in the correct order to complete the sentence.

Painting is messy, b u t it is fun!

u b t

38

not

Say the word. Then trace the word.

not not not not

Write the word.

Begin at the red arrow. Connect the dots to finish the picture.

Complete the maze. Color the circles that have the word not.

Cut out the letters at the bottom of the page. Then paste them in the correct order to complete the sentence.

She is n o t hungry.

o n t

39

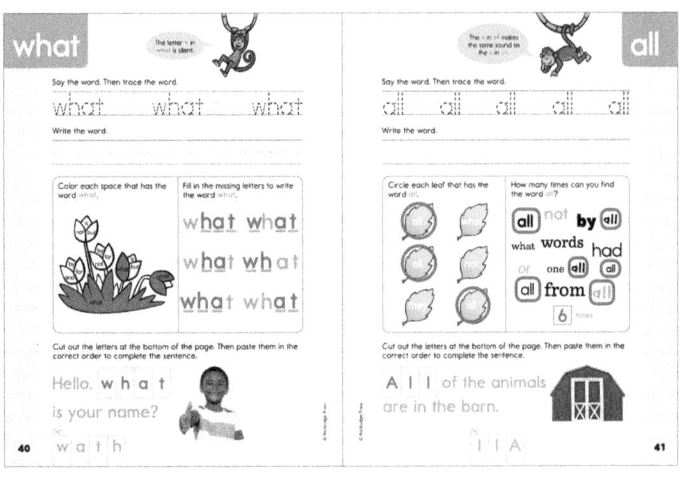
what

Say the word. Then trace the word.

what what what

Write the word.

Color each space that has the word what.

Fill in the missing letters to write the word what.

what what what what what what

Cut out the letters at the bottom of the page. Then paste them in the correct order to complete the sentence.

Hello, w h a t is your name?

w a t h

40

all

Say the word. Then trace the word.

all all all all all

Write the word.

Circle each leaf that has the word all.

How many times can you find the word all?

6 times

Cut out the letters at the bottom of the page. Then paste them in the correct order to complete the sentence.

A l l of the animals are in the barn.

l l A

41

were

Say the word. Then trace the word.

were were were

Write the word.

Draw a line to match each word.

Find and circle the word were three times.

Cut out the letters at the bottom of the page. Then paste them in the correct order to complete the sentence.

The horses w e r e running earlier.

e r w e

42

we

Say the word. Then trace the word.

we we we we we

Write the word.

Color each space that has the word we.

Find the word we. Draw a line to connect the letters.

Cut out the letters at the bottom of the page. Then paste them in the correct order to complete the sentence.

W e like to jump rope.

e W

43

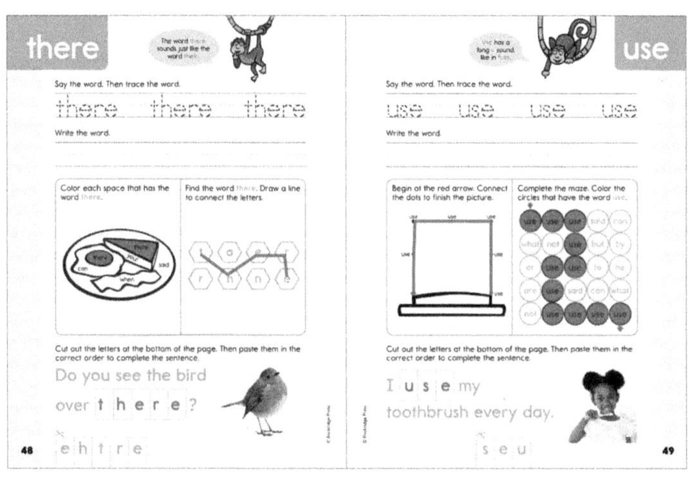
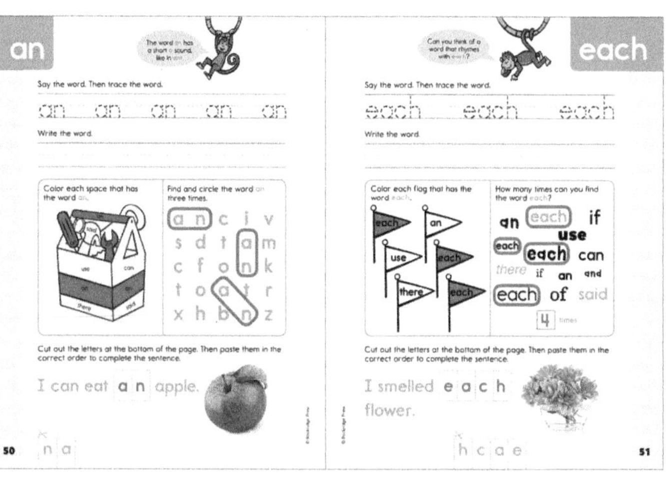
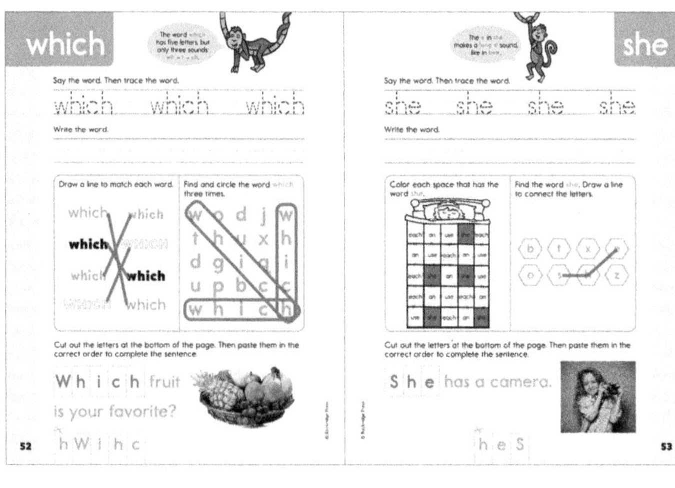
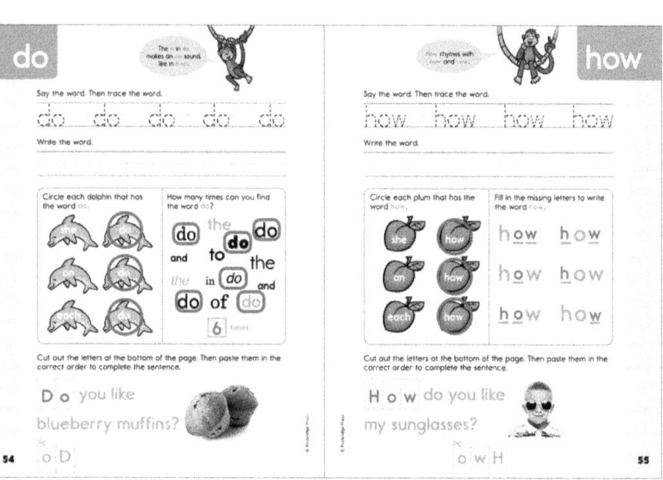

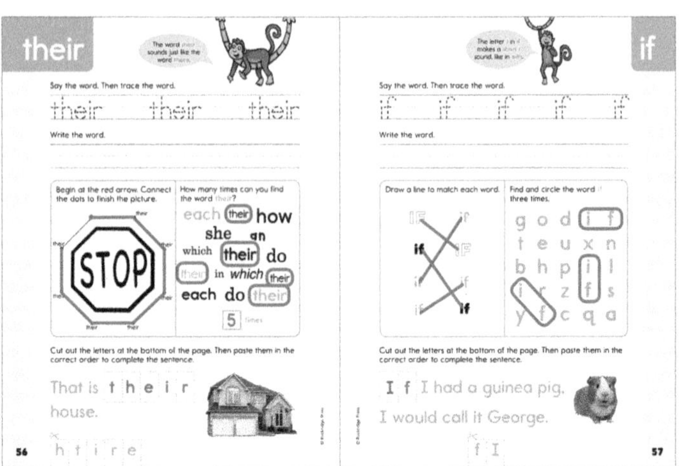

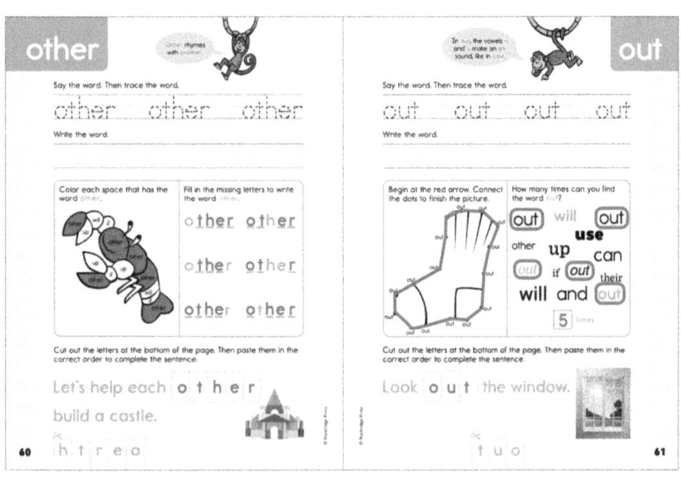
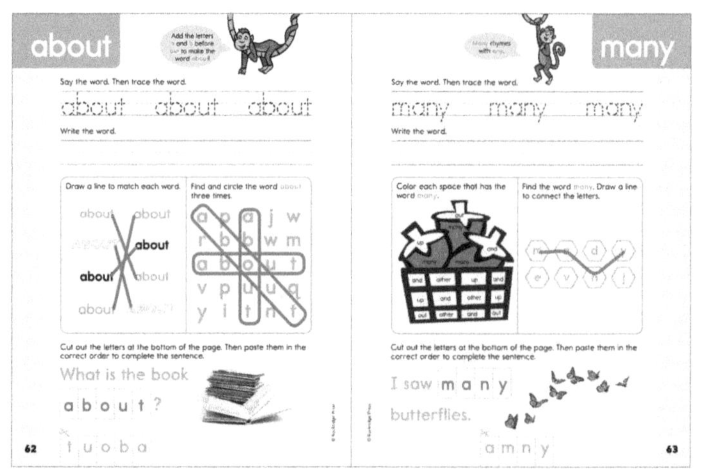

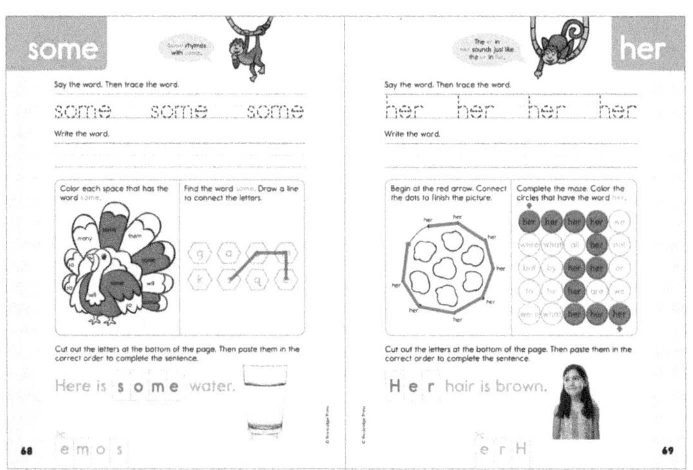
some
her
some some some
her her her her
Here is some water.
Her hair is brown.
68
69

would
make
would would would
make make make
I would like a banana.
Let's make cupcakes!
70
71

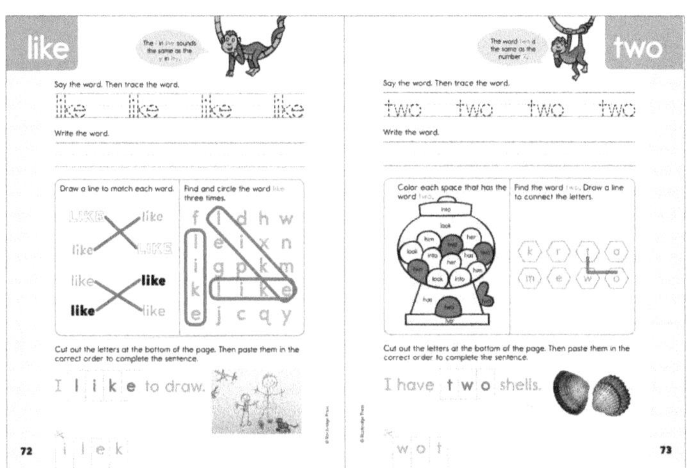
like
two
like like like like
two two two two
I like to draw.
I have two shells.
72
73

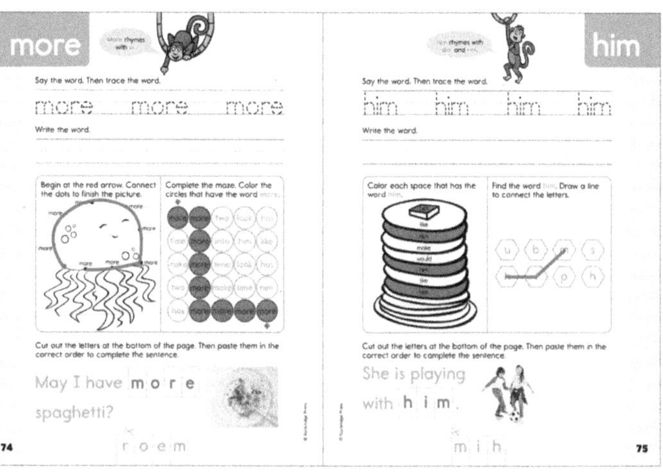
more
him
more more more
him him him him
May I have more spaghetti?
She is playing with him.
74
75

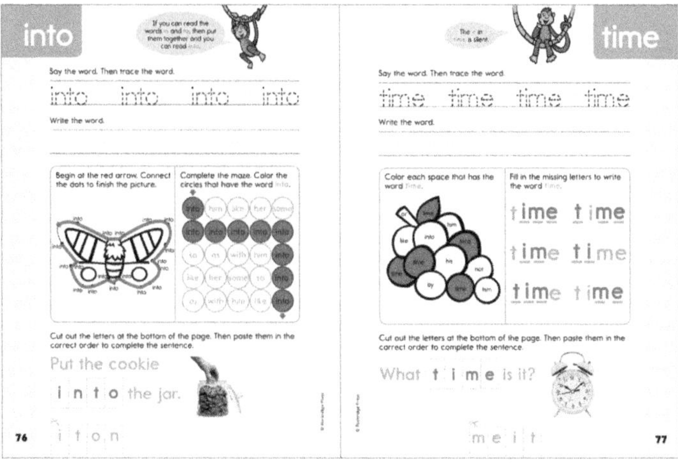
into
time
into into into into
time time time time
Put the cookie into the jar.
What time is it?
76
77

has
look
has has has has
look look look look
He has a guitar.
Look what she can do!
78
79

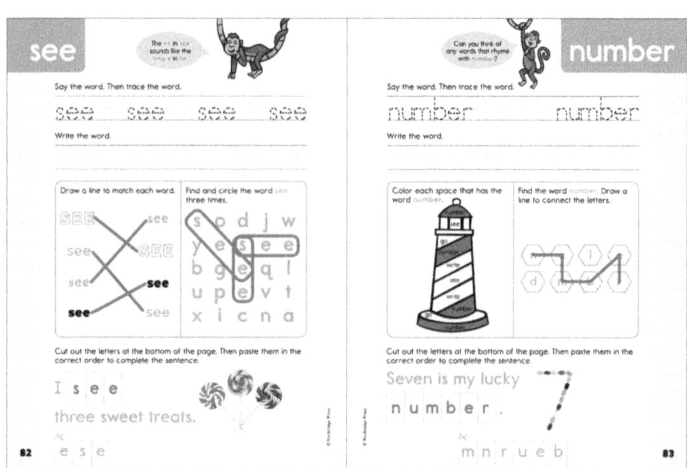

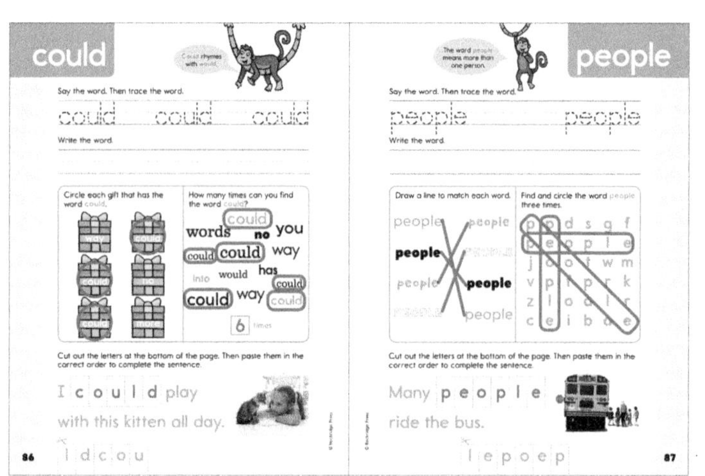
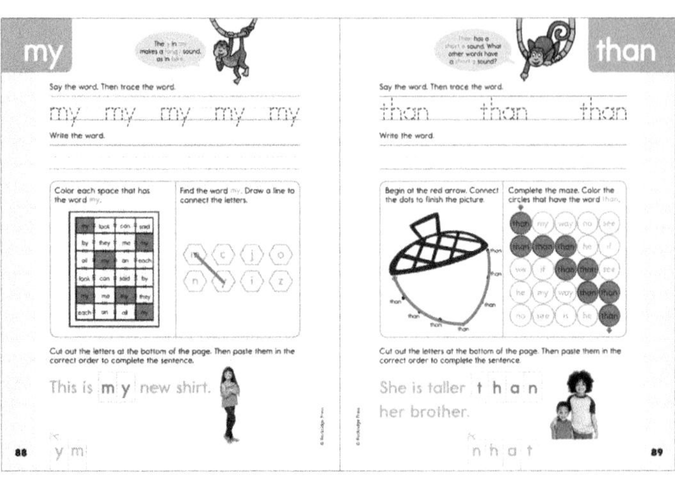
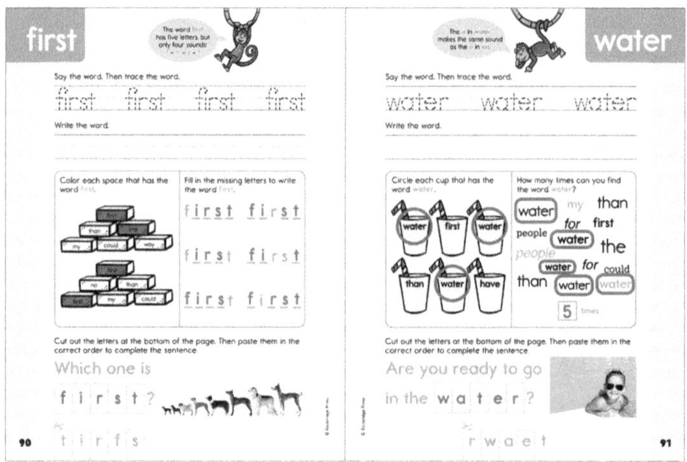

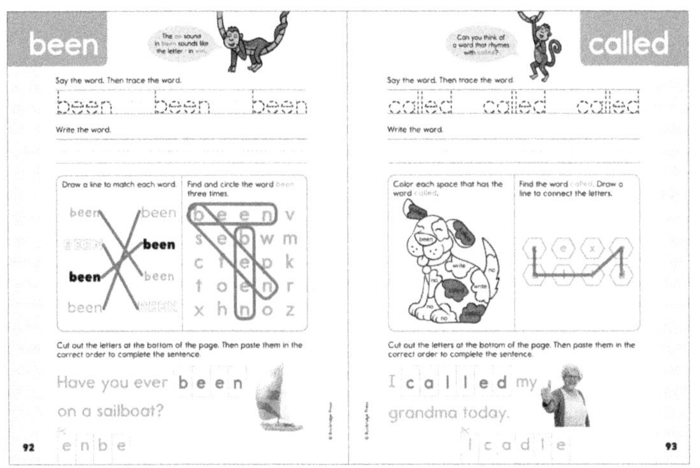
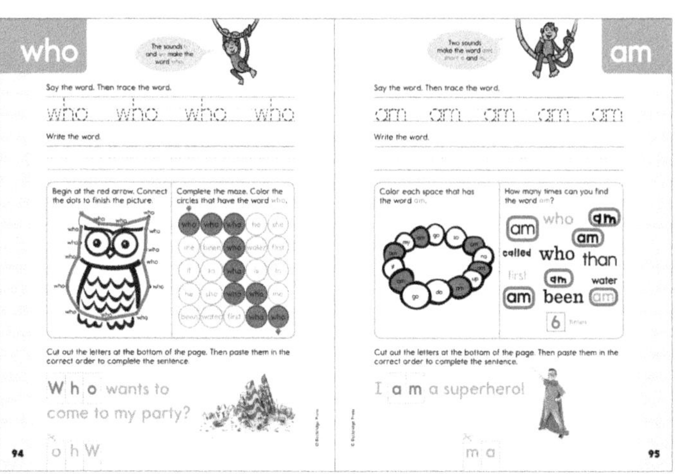
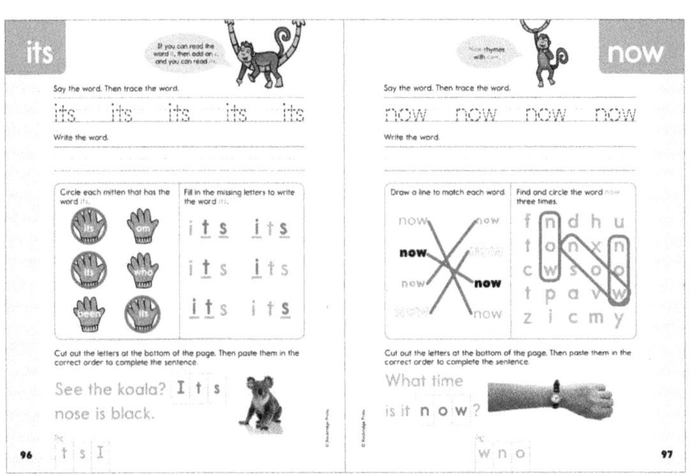
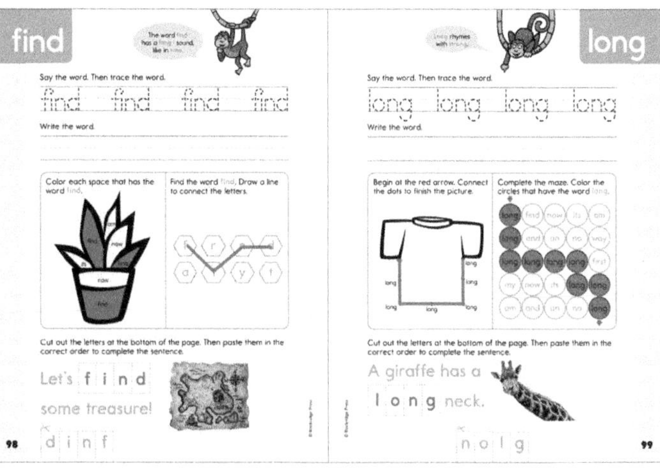
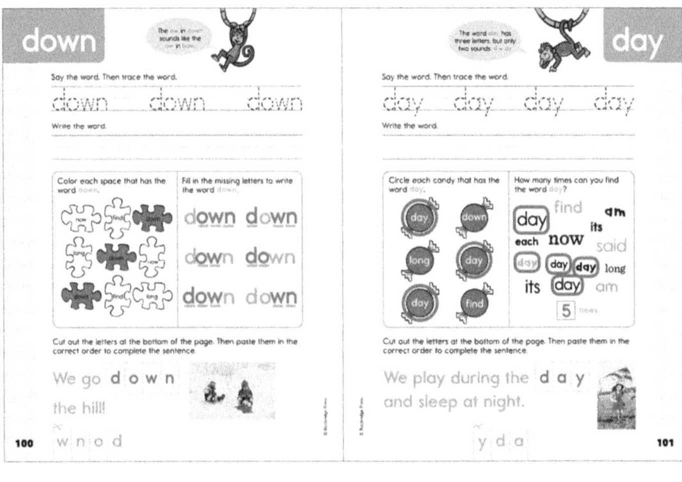
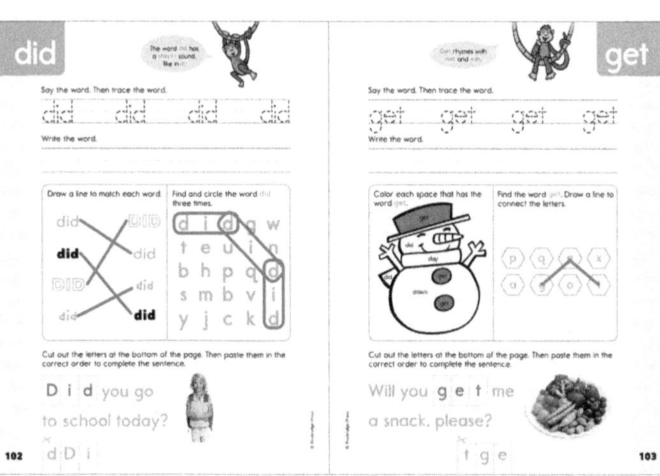

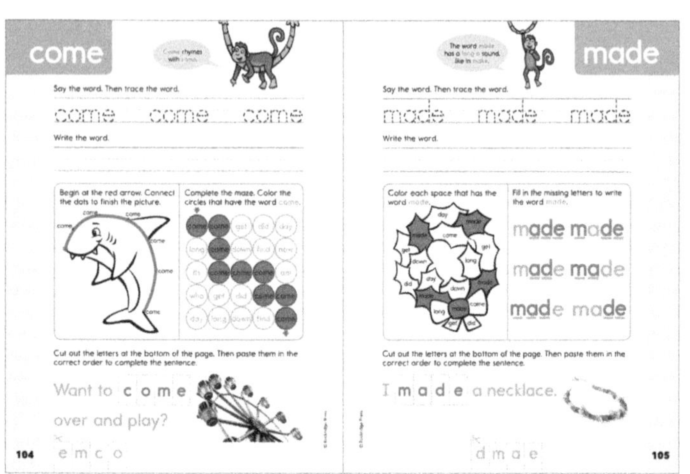
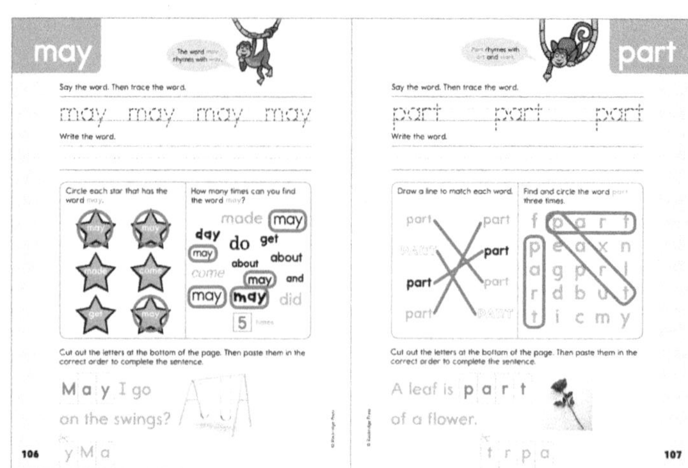
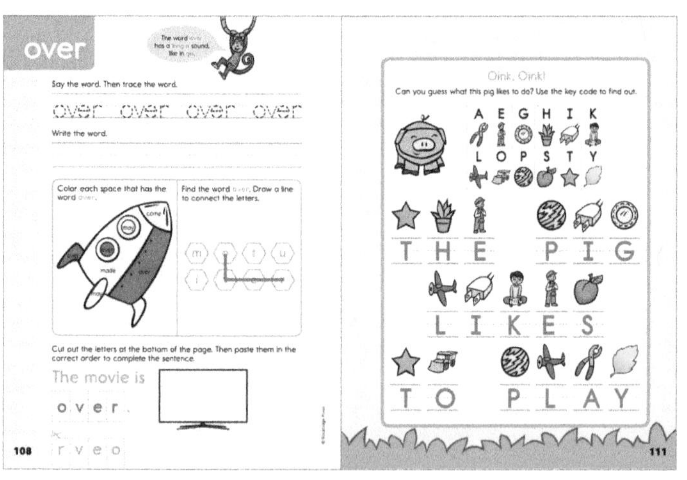
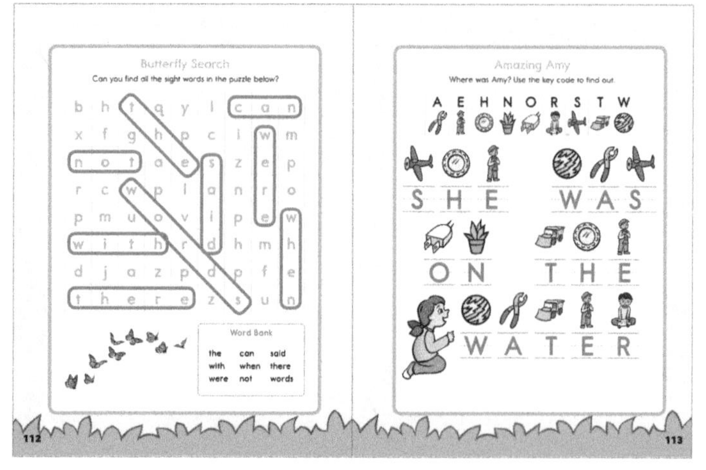
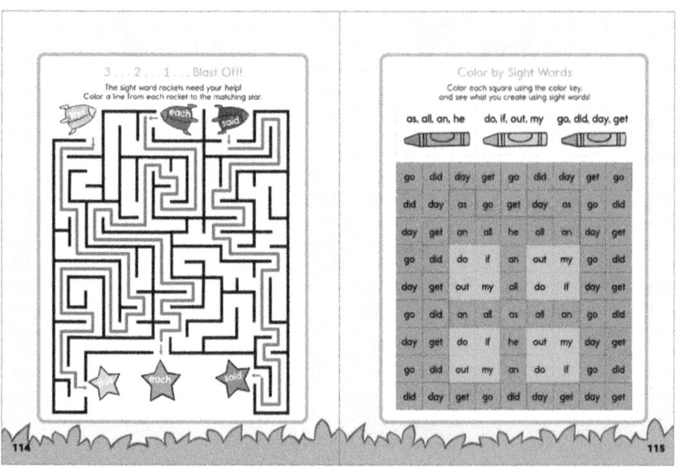

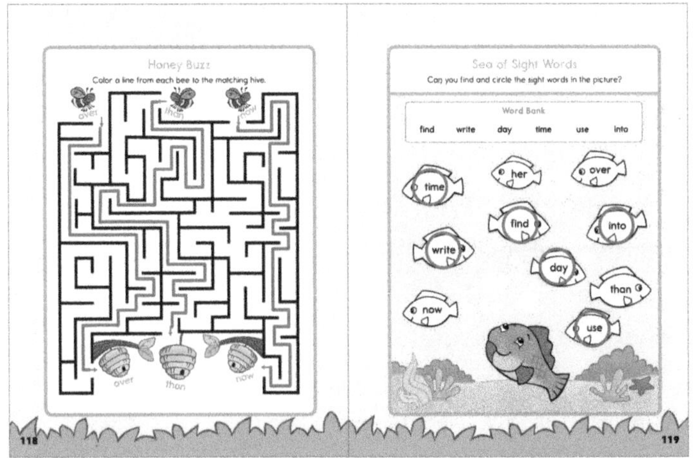

Honey Buzz

Color a line from each bee to the matching hive.

over than now

over than now

118

Sea of Sight Words

Can you find and circle the sight words in the picture?

Word Bank

find write day time use into

time her over find into write day than now use

119

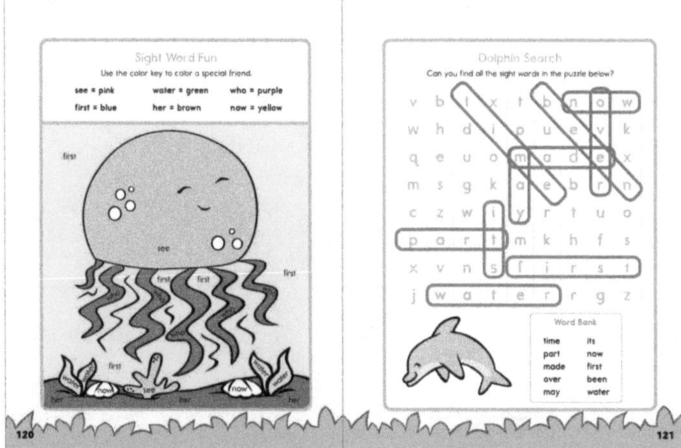

Sight Word Fun

Use the color key to color a special friend.

see = pink water = green who = purple
first = blue her = brown now = yellow

120

Dolphin Search

Can you find all the sight words in the puzzle below?

v b i x t b n o w
w h d i p u e v k
q e u o m a d e x
m s g k a e b r n
c z w i y r t u o
p a r t m k h f s
x v n s f i r s t
j w a t e r r g z

Word Bank

time its
part now
made first
over been
may water

121

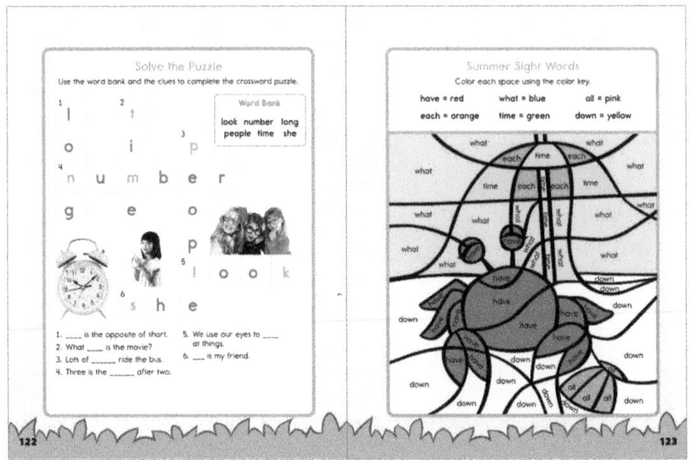

Solve the Puzzle

Use the word bank and the clues to complete the crossword puzzle.

Word Bank

look number long
people time she

1. ____ is the opposite of short.
2. What ____ is the movie?
3. Lots of ______ ride the bus.
4. Three is the ______ after two.
5. We use our eyes to ____ at things.
6. ___ is my friend.

122

Summer Sight Words

Color each space using the color key.

have = red what = blue all = pink
each = orange time = green down = yellow

123

Author Bio

Laurin Brainard, MEd, is the founder of ThePrimaryBrain.com. Through her blog, Laurin shares teaching ideas, fun activities, crafts, and curriculum ideas. Laurin is the mother of preschoolers, a first-grade teacher, and a curriculum designer for The Primary Brain. When she isn't teaching or designing curricula, Laurin enjoys making memories with her family.

You are on your way to becoming a reader!

____

has completed all the activities in

My Sight Words Workbook.

YOU ARE A SIGHT WORDS SUPERSTAR!

CPSIA information can be obtained
at www.ICGtesting.com
Printed in the USA
LVHW052057270320
651336LV00002B/2

9 781641 525862